Summer Restoration

Rosie Dresser and The Cobbler's

"This white Colonial frame house,
Willed downward, Dear, from you to us
Still matters . . ."

Robert Lowell, "Fourth of July in Maine"
from *The Ocean*

Summer Restoration

Rosie Dresser and The Cobbler's

JOCK HERRON

Jock Herron

TIDEPOOL PRESS
Cambridge, Massachusetts

Published in the United States in 2004 by TidePool Press

For information, address TidePool Press,
6 Maple Avenue, Cambridge, Massachusetts 02139
www.tidepoolpress.com

Designed by Ingrid Mach
Manufactured in the United States of America

Library of Congress Cataloging-in-Publication Data

Herron, Jock 1951-
Summer Restoration: Rosie Dresser and The Cobbler's
p. cm.
Includes bibliographical references
ISBN 0-9755557-0-7
1. Rose Lincoln Dresser (1909-1991) 2. Somesville and Mt. Desert, Maine
3. Theater 4. Red Cross—World War II 5. Winsor School 6. Worcester, Massachusetts 7. New England—Social History I. Title

2004094513

Summer Restoration: Rosie Dresser and The Cobbler's is written with her great nephews and nieces most in mind. They are the fourth generation to enjoy the house and the fifth to enjoy the island of Mt. Desert. In ascending order of age, you are:

Benjamin Nathaniel Richardson
Levi Lincoln Winsor Herron
Samuel Richard Dresser
Winslow Sever Dresser
Caleb Jackson Dresser
Edward Winslow Herron
Stephen Merrick Herron
Samuel Bradford Truesdell
Andrew Clarke Herron
Jill Anne Dresser
Amy Elizabeth Dresser

Rose Lincoln Dresser on the path at Jordan Pond,
Mt. Desert Island, Maine (late 1980s)

TABLE OF CONTENTS

"Heritage. Nostalgia. Freighted words—nostalgia especially, a term itself subject to reinterpretation over time. Pejorative today, implying a distorted vision to be avoided, but a term that carried a clear and precise meaning once in the eighteenth century: 'homesickness'. German *Heimweh*, a condition recognized as requiring treatment and, thus, when diagnosed in a soldier, entitling him to a spell of home leave."

Penelope Lively, *A House Unlocked*

INTRODUCTION

Ostensibly, this short book is about the restoration of a small house in a tiny village on the coast of Maine during the summer of 1947. That certainly is the focal point of the fourteen letters Rosie Dresser sent home that summer describing her progress in transforming *The Cobbler's* from a decrepit old building into a graceful summer house on the main street of Somesville, a quiet harbor village at the head of Somes Sound on Mt. Desert Island. The story, however, is scarcely about chimneys and kitchens, plaster and paint. It is about Rosie herself, an unmarried thirty-eight year old Vassar dropout just back from the war who was returning, on new and independent terms, to a community she had known from childhood summers. It is also about the village of Somesville, an old coastal town on the cusp of change.

When Rosie returned to Somesville in 1947, the village was as close in spirit to the late 1860s as it was to the late 1960s. Several incidents in the letters bear that out:

–When Rosie found a dead man's dentures in the attic, her contractor convinced her to give them to his toothless assistant rather than throw them away.

–The proprietress of the rooming house where Rosie initially stayed while *The Cobbler's* was being restored dropped by for an afternoon to help peel off ancient layers of crusty wallpaper with her fruit knife.

–After asking Rosie if she would be willing to help dress a dead body, the local undertaker, who was also the village grocer, assured her that, "Bodies can't do ya no harm. It's the live ones that are bothersome."

Unreflectively but with great warmth, Rosie captures the local characters just as she knew them—colorful, wry, prickly, resourceful, kind. Her letters offer a glimpse into a gritty, vulnerable culture about to be softened by some of the homogenizing forces of post-war America: television, the turnpike, jet planes, the power saw, fiberglass. Life in Somesville changed quickly between 1947 and, say, 1967.

The world had already changed for Rosie, particularly between 1938 when she spent a year living with cousins in Greece and 1946 when she returned from the frontlines of war. She had grown up in a traditional Yankee family, spent the war years with the Red Cross and returned a different person—better organized, less sheltered, more appreciative of the quotidian aspects of life. In many respects, 1947 was a liberating year for her—a chance to move forward and backward at the same time. In restoring *The Cobbler's*, she moved back to the Maine of her childhood summers, but on fresh terms as a single, well-educated woman striking out on her own. This story pivots around that summer, a seminal one for Rosie who—like the country as a whole—was putting her life back on track.

The letters resurfaced when the director of the Worcester

Art Museum asked if Rosie's sister—the art historian Louisa Dresser—had left any files describing her 1938 visit to the excavation of Antioch which was jointly sponsored by the Louvre and the Worcester, Baltimore and Princeton University museums. More accomplished at saving letters than protecting capital, the Dressers had accumulated a seventy-thousand piece archive collection running from the late eighteenth century deep into the twentieth. Catalogued by professional archivists, it is an eclectic collection that includes party invitations from the 1920s, war letters from world wars one and two, diaries of an Antiguan plantation family, letters from Jefferson and other prominent politicians, a young girl's account of court life in Madrid, photograph albums dating back to the 1870s, account books, ancient diplomas, house plans and estate settlements. As it turned out, there was only one letter from Louisa describing her visit to Antioch. But, sifting through the seven boxes dedicated to her, I came across a manila folder with these fourteen letters written by Rosie in 1947. Misfiling, it turns out, has its virtues.

Switching gears quickly from the Middle East to Down East, I spent several hours absorbed by the story she told of restoring a house her nephews and nieces still own and love in a community that has changed materially, but not yet beyond recognition. It seemed like a story worth sharing.

The letters themselves have more anthropological than artistic value. The content is beguiling, but the prose, itself, is erratic. In some ways this is surprising. Somesville, during the early 1950s, attracted a remarkable number of talented writers who happened to be women—Helen Howe, Marguerite Yourcenar and her translator Grace Frick, Margaret Ayer Barnes, Marian Lawrence Peabody—but Rosie, who was a friend of each, had neither their patience nor literary gift. She dashed these letters off, quickly making her point and moving on. Rosie's real talent—and it shows up in these letters—was her natural ability to connect to the local people who helped her that summer and who became her friends, individually and collectively, over the rest of their lives. Using simple and unpretentious anecdote, these letters capture the local character—the humor, language and lives —of the "Maine-iacs", as Rosie affectionately referred to her new generation of friends in Somesville.

Just back from the war and enamored of the local Maine dialect, Rosie uses a colloquial style that becomes contrived at points. An actress by training and pursuit, she should have recorded these letters. Anyone who knew Rosie will easily imagine her performing what she has written—capturing the dialect in her rich voice, mimicking facial expressions and using a room and a few props to make each story and each character come alive. While the letters more than stand on their own, anyone reading them who knew Rosie will have the added pleasure of imagining her voice—comic, distinct, and always "in character".

The letters benefit from some context. The first two chapters describe Rosie's life prior to 1947, and the third does the same for Somesville and the island of Mount Desert. Chapter Four consists of the letters themselves and a supporting commentary. The final chapter, an epilogue, traces the last four decades of Rosie's life.

The letters are transcribed *verbatim*. Read in sequence, they tell a story entirely on their own. But I have briefly introduced each one—adding context, amplifying themes, noting quirky connections, highlighting particular anecdotes, pursuing tangents. The reader may not lose much if she goes straight to the letters and simply reads them sequentially with no editorial embellishment. That is exactly what I did.

"The past is never dead. It's not even past."

William Faulkner, *Requiem for a Nun*

chapter ONE

Rosie Dresser and Her Family

RLD in an Alice-in-Wonderland pose (circa 1918)

The Lincoln-Dresser Family

Rose Lincoln Dresser was born on October 9, 1909 in Worcester, Massachusetts, into the sort of inbred, self-absorbed New England family that flourished a century ago, but which, like an archaic species, became more or less extinct during the Permian turmoil of two world wars and the Depression. Rosie was the second of four children and the second daughter born to Josephine Rose Lincoln and Frank Farnum Dresser. Although her parents, as her grandparents had before them, lived in Europe for several years, the family never strayed far physically or psychically from Central Massachusetts and two original outposts of Massachusetts: Mt. Desert, Maine and Woodstock, Connecticut.

It is hard to understand Rosie and even harder to appreciate her independence without having a sense of her family. Several aspects come quickly to mind: Although well engaged in the present, ancestral reverence ran deep; although world travelers, geographic primacy for many generations was narrowly confined to Worcester, Woodstock, and the state of Maine; although historically patriarchal, a twentieth century matriarchy began to emerge during the early years of Rosie's childhood. Each point is worth considering.

Rose L. Dresser and Her Family

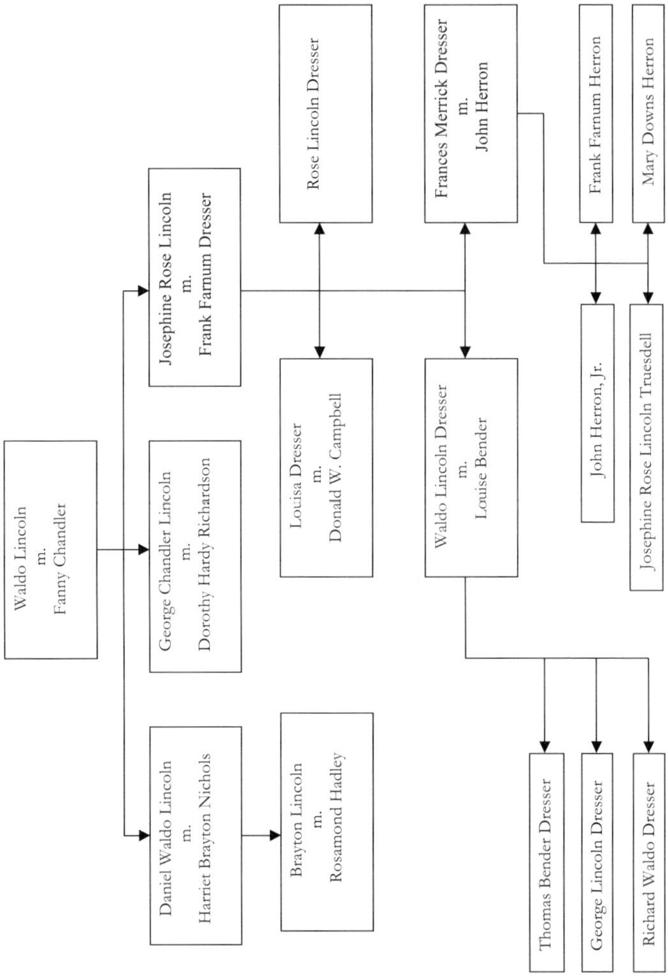

Like a colony of ancestrally devoted lab rats, Rosie's family was deeply inbred but—unlike the rats—they knew how to keep genetic score. When her uncle, George Chandler Lincoln, married Dorothy Hardy Richardson in 1921, a wedding guest whispered, "This makes George my first, second and third cousin." Rosie's younger sister, Frannie, wrote and lectured about two prominent ancestral Tories, Timothy Paine and John Chandler III, who—she enjoyed noting—had a complex relationship: the former being simultaneously the son-in-law and stepson of the latter. According to a well-researched genealogical chart, Rosie was descended from William and Annis Chandler through six separate ancestral lines. Other progenitors make multiple appearances on the radial chart as well. Rosie was her own cousin many times over.

Genealogy rather than tennis or golf was the family game. Rosie's grandfather, Waldo Lincoln, celebrated himself by writing the Waldo and the Lincoln genealogies. The former was eleven-hundred pages, the latter seven- hundred. Luckily for him, he had no middle name. Rosie's great-grandfather, Dr. George Chandler, wrote the thirteen-hundred page Chandler genealogy and her cousin, Nathaniel Paine, wrote the mercifully short twenty-five page Paine genealogy. Never married, Rosie turned her genealogical knowledge on its head. When asked once why she remained single, she answered simply, "The Lincolns always marry above themselves, and I've never met anyone better than I am."

The Lincoln family of Rosie's childhood were New England Shintoists, inexhaustibly devoted to their ancestors.

Saving thousands of family letters and other ephemera is a modest example. More strikingly—especially for an impressionable young girl—over forty iconic family portraits dating from the mid-eighteenth century hung in the house of Waldo and Fanny Lincoln, Rosie's grandparents. Interestingly, nearly half were of women. All remain in the family today except for two eighteenth century pastels that were destroyed in a house fire in 1984.

The portraits were a constant reminder of the family's storied past, although with each passing generation they began to represent—as Oppenheimer said of the later Einstein—"monuments rather than beacons." Rosie's mother, Josephine Rose Lincoln, was from a distinguished political family that included four Massachusetts governors, one governor of Maine, two governors of Virginia, two mayors of Worcester, Jefferson's attorney general, a president of the Boston & Albany Railroad, several justices of the Massachusetts courts and a slew of provincial eighteenth century Tories who held a "dizzying array of positions" that reached "epic proportions" according to a recent Massachusetts historian. Most of the latter were forced to leave Massachusetts for England and Canada in 1783. Rosie's father, Frank Farnum Dresser, was a prominent Worcester lawyer who had grown up in the household of his kinsman Senator George Frisbie Hoar, excellent preparation for living with his wife's self-absorbed family.

Rosie's family was rooted in central Massachusetts for upwards of ten generations. In a talk given in 1952 to the Worcester Fire Society, Rosie's uncle and future benefactor,

George Chandler Lincoln, noted:

> My father, Waldo Lincoln, was an antiquarian and he often said to me that it was a curious fact that some families, even for generations, were on the move. They were Goers. The Waldos, he said, were migrators as a rule. The Lincolns, on the contrary, were usually happy to stay put. They were Stayers.

Rosie's family was firmly on the side of the "Stayers". Although they were, and had been for several generations, world travelers, the family—both immediate and extended—stayed very close to home. And Worcester—where at least eleven streets were named after them: Chandler, Salisbury, Paine, Lincoln, Waldo, Sever, Merrick, Orne, Winslow, Farnum, Pelham—was home. They even tended to stay in the same house over many generations. Seven generations of Lincolns lived in the Lincoln Mansion at 49 Elm Street before it was moved in 1951 to the entrance of Old Sturbridge Village. In Pomfret, Connecticut—just across the border and once part of Massachusetts—some ten successive generations of Chandlers had lived at Chandler Farms. Rosie inherited an elegant, 1757 embroidery that shows the house at Chandler Farms, a loving wedding couple, a complicit Cupid and several black servants.

Even when the family moved—Rosie's Uncle George and Aunt Dorothy Lincoln to live in Woodstock, Connecticut and her parents to Mt. Desert for the summers—they landed in places with old family ties. Woodstock was founded by the Chandlers in 1637, and dominated by them for many

Frances Merrick Lincoln—lover of horses, buildings, paintings and great-nieces (circa 1890)

years afterwards. Seemingly distant, Maine and Mt. Desert were also in Rosie's blood. In 1808, Rosie's relative, Salem Towne, Jr., made the first land survey of Mt. Desert. Eighteen years later, another relative, Enoch Lincoln, became the third governor of Maine. Enoch wrote *The Village* (1816), the first poem published in Maine, and mastered local Indian dialects for his historical research. Salem Towne was commemorated at *The Cobbler's* by a trivet of the *Salem Towne House* sold as a souvenir by Old Sturbridge Village where the house stands today. Rosie enjoyed quoting Harrison Gray Otis who claimed that his fellow Massachusetts legislator, Salem Towne, "should have been named Marblehead". Enoch

Lincoln was celebrated more substantially at *The Cobbler's* by a Chester Harding portrait hung in the living room and an engraving at the front door.

During the early twentieth century the family began morphing from a patriarchy into a matriarchy, an evolution that may explain much of Rosie's independence. Her great aunt, Frances Merrick Lincoln, was an especially formidable woman who never married. Among other things, she was a long-term trustee of the Worcester Lunatic Asylum—despite its regressive name, a comparatively progressive institution—and an original trustee of the Worcester Art Museum where she headed the Building Committee, back then an unusual assignment for a woman. In her case, however, it was quite fitting. Having inherited much of the Lincoln family land around Elm Street, she built a number of houses on speculation. She was so successful as a businesswoman and so active in public works, that it did not surprise her family when they heard that a streetcar driver passing her on a Worcester street had announced to his passengers, "That's Miss Lincoln. She oughta be Mayor." Her father, Daniel Waldo Lincoln, and her grandfather, Levi Lincoln II, had been just that.

The legacy of the Great-Aunt Frances—and her strong willed predecessors like Anne Hutchinson, Rebecca Nurse and Penelope Winslow Sever Lincoln—was keenly felt by the next two generations of women in the family. Rosie's mother, known as Ga, was widowed at forty-nine with four children in 1924. She responded to her husband's tragically early death with Yankee resilience rather than self-pity. In addition to raising her four children, she became actively involved in the civic life of Worcester. She was president of the Worcester Children's Friend Society, president of the Bancroft School, president of the Worcester Player's Club and was appointed by Massachusetts Governor Alvan Fuller as a trustee of the Worcester Lunatic Asylum—all typically male roles in the early to mid-twentieth century.

RLD and sister Louisa with President Taft and British Ambassador Lord Bryce in front of 49 Elm where they had spent the night as guests of Waldo Lincoln, then president of the American Antiquarian Society (1912)

By the summer of 1947 when Rosie was writing these letters, her elder sister Louisa had already written what James Thomas Flexner would later call a "magisterial catalogue" of seventeenth-century American portraits, "a lonely tower among the flimsy study of our early art." Louisa was well on her way to becoming one of the pre-eminent historians of early American art. She was the curator of collections at the Worcester Art Museum where she had served as acting director during the second world war. In addition to the matriarchal role models whom she lived with as a child, Rosie grew up surrounded by the previously mentioned collection of forty family portraits hanging throughout 49 Elm. Almost half were women. Rosie, it is fair to say, came by her matriarchal independence early and honestly.

Rosie Dresser

Rosie's life had a rich arc: a privileged New England childhood; a fine education in the United States and abroad; a fling on the New York stage; several years owning and operating a summer stock theater; a year in Greece before the Second World War; three years in Europe and the Philippines with the Red Cross during the war; a twenty-four year teaching career at the Winsor School in Boston; a year teaching in Florence at the Villa Mercedi; nearly two decades as an actress and a director with the Foothills Theater Company in Worcester.

But that quick outline misses much. There were certainly hardships. Her father, Frank Farnum Dresser, died unexpectedly in Worcester of Bright's disease in 1924 while the rest of the family was living in the south of France. A decade later, the Dressers were caught unprepared for the Depression, and only survived it in some comfort because an extended network of Lincoln and Dresser parents, aunts, uncles and cousins provided support to Rosie's mother—paying tuitions, helping maintain the old house and eventually providing inheritances that made life easier. Although Rosie was nominally a "recreation volunteer" in the Red Cross during the war, she was in the early wave of Americans to enter the death camps of Europe. She never discussed the raw brutality she saw in those camps until the very end of her life. Nor did she ever marry. That may not have been a hardship, but when her 65-year old elder sister married for the first time in 1971, Rosie seemed very conflicted about it.

On the other hand, those challenges—especially during the Depression—seemed to fortify her. She was ready for anything, and took the cliché of "living life to the fullest" to a daily extreme: she awoke at 5:30, or earlier, every morning and was on the go until midnight or later. She rarely slept. She either gave or went to cocktail parties and dinners four or five nights a week. She was deeply involved with organizations in Worcester, Boston and Somesville: the Shakespeare Club, the First Unitarian Church, the Bancroft School, the Thursday Club and the Players Club in Worcester; the Winsor School in Boston; the Somesville Landing Corporation and the Village Improvement Society in Maine.

But we are skipping too quickly into the story. When Rosie wrote these letters in the summer of 1947 she was thirty-eight years old, and just back from the war. Although much lay ahead, she had already experienced a rich life—especially for a young woman of that time. Her childhood—described below in her own hand—had prepared her improbably well for the uncertainties of war. As her short sketch of growing up at 49 Elm suggests, flexibility, resourcefulness and good humor were in abundant supply. The family had too much spunk to slip into morose despair as their privileged world became unhinged.

49 Elm Street, Worcester, Massachusetts

49 Elm Street by Rose Lincoln Dresser

My sister, Frannie Herron, who writes extremely well and is also a competent scholar, and my other sister, Louisa Dresser, an *eminent* scholar and art historian, have said many times over the years: "The story of 49 Elm Street must be told!" I am neither a writer nor a scholar, but I am going to jot down my recollections lest none more important ever get recorded.

In 1836, Levi Lincoln, Jr. moved from his house at the corner of Elm and Main Streets (where the old Poli's theatre later stood) and *fait accompli* '49' was erected. The architect was Elias Carter. The house was dubbed *Oregon*, because it was so far west from the center of Worcester. Levi's son, Daniel Waldo Lincoln, inherited it. He left it to his son, Waldo, who vacated it in 1919 at the birth of my younger sister Frannie Dresser. All the Dressers were crammed into 26 Fruit Street: Father, Mother, Louisa, Rosie, Waldo, Frannie – not to mention Nellie and Peggy and Nannie, acquisitions from Ireland and Scotland. After savoring a winter in California and a few years in an apartment at 46 Elm, Waldo and his wife, Fanny, moved into the newly erected little brick house built in the grove at '49'. At my father's death, they moved back to '49' and endured the growing pains of four grandchildren. Granny Lincoln's illness made it necessary for her to be at the McLean's Hospital, and I think Grandfather rather enjoyed the activities of the young. He was very popular with all our friends and they all called him "Grandfather".

The morning of my tenth birthday, October 9, 1919, I walked along Fruit Street to the corner of Elm. I was pushing a doll carriage crammed with my dolls "Polly" and "Florence" and an odd teddy or two. I paused dramatically and looked back at #26 and said: "That is the house where I spent my

The Dresser children—Louisa, Waldo, RLD and Frannie on the side steps of 49 Elm (early 1920s)

childhood. My childhood is over." I pursued my way up Elm Street, vans charging past me loaded with furniture, etc., etc., etc. and was delighted to discover on arrival that I had been assigned to the bedroom at the head of the stairs because I was the neater of the two girls and Louisa was given the room less evident. Mother and Daddy had the front east room and the first west room was for guests. Nannie, Franny and Waldo had the three rooms in one ell and Nellie, Peggy and a new acquisition, Dela, had the three rooms in the back ell - with only one radiator in the hall! No comforts for the employees in my grandfather's planning. Each of us had a radiator apiece and there were five fireplaces on the second floor

The library at 49 Elm, facing south (late 1940s)

that Thompson lit on cold mornings. All the bathtubs were tin – and no porcelain tub has ever been so warm and cozy. We soon settled in. It was a longer walk to school —but it was nearer Green's Drug Store on Main Street and Jimmy's Ice Cream Emporium on the corner of West and Pleasant.

Our first Christmas at 49 Elm was fabulous. When we went downstairs at dawn on December 25, we could not believe our eyes. The presents stretched from the fireplace two-thirds of the length of the library. Our mother, Josephine Rose, was no slouch as a Santa. She had investigated the attic and had produced all the Doll House furniture of her era, not to mention Granny Lincoln's; all the soldiers and toy villages belonging to Uncles Merrick, Dan and George; a few dolls of Dorothy's and paper dolls galore. No Christmas has ever been so exciting!

The attic was full of marvelous treasures. Anything could be found there. One time when Louisa was going to Europe and North Africa, Mother gave a dinner party in her honor. She thought suitable decorations might be found in the attic and she was right. Nannie and Zita waited on table wearing fezes on their heads and the centerpiece represented Egypt. Mother had found a box saying "Sand from the Sahara" and a bottle labeled "Water from the River Jordan".

I recall the doorbell ringing one evening and Bill Whipple announcing he was going to a costume party as Bottom and by chance did we have the head of an ass in the attic. We did.

One day, my mother was preparing for a Thursday Club and the house had an unusual "spic and span" look. While mother was in the kitchen supervising the goodies, Louisa, who was doing props for a Players Club show arrived with a truck and moved out a table and a couple of chairs. Mother returned to the Library to view the vacancies. Nothing daunted her. She summoned Thompson who went to the attic and produced replacements. While she was upstairs, I arrived with another truck and removed a picture, a couple of statues and a bit of furniture for a play at the Bancroft School. Thompson and the attic again to the rescue and Mother had the damage repaired by twelve o'clock!

'49' always seemed to be connected to theatricals of various sorts. One evening our cousin Betsy Barton came to the front door looking for the rehearsal of a play to be given by the Unitarian church. She went into the front parlor and found a group of thespians who proved to be rehearsing for the Shakespeare Club "Revels". She tried the library and there was the Players Club group. They waved her on to the dining room, and there she found her cast.

One evening Frannie returned from New Haven and went upstairs to bed. The next morning she was awakened by strange bangings and stomps and the beat, beat, beat of the piano. On descending, she discovered the Junior League chorus was preparing for a gala show.

49 Elm was a wonderful house for parties. I was brought up on the tale of Levi and his wife sitting calmly in the parlor, awaiting the arrival of their dinner guest, the captain of the militia currently billeted in Worcester. In the distance was heard the trump, trump, trump of soldiers. The captain had misinterpreted "the pleasure of your company is requested for dinner". His entire company was at hand. The host blanched, but his lady said calmly, "Don't worry, my dear, entertain the gentleman for a short while and I will see that there is enough for all." Grandfather used to taunt Mother and say, "What would you have done with such a problem?" Mother always replied calmly, "Why I'd call the Worcester Club and summon Mr. Scott."

The Worcester Club rescued us on many occasions. Louisa's coming out party was the biggest and best of our generation's festivities. A large tea was held in the afternoon and quantities of elderly ladies in garden party hats arrived. Before the dance in the evening, the aunts and uncles were host to a dinner at the Club. Waldo, Frannie and I did not attend that event. Before the gala group returned for the dance, a young man who had not been at the dance arrived a half hour early. Nannie summoned me and forced me to entertain him in the garden among the swinging Japanese lanterns. Waldo was posted at his bedroom window and reported to Nannie, "I kept waiting for him to say these 'forever and ever' words, but he didn't." Frannie's reaction

The library at 49 Elm, facing north (late 1940s)

to the coming out party was different. Some time after it we were summoned to Aunt Frances' house to watch the night blooming *cereus* bloom. We were all sitting in silence waiting for the great unfolding when young Frannie, in a stage whisper, asked Nannie: "Is this Auntie's giving-out party?"

Frannie's coming out party was apparently a wow. I was living in Greece, so missed it, but I received many vivid accounts. The Big Apple was all the rage that year. Just before the party Mother had a dreadful thought, so she summoned Mr. Lowell to investigate the floor. Naturally, he had to shore up the foundations. Otherwise, an entire generation of beauties and their beaux might have disappeared. At the height of the festivities, my Aunt Emma, sitting in state observing the fun, was approached by two young men who said, "What's going on here? What's this party all about?" She summoned Waldo who discovered they were unknown Worcester Tech boys who had dropped by to investigate the excitement. He urged them to stay and kept them busy all evening by introducing them to some of the problem debs. The climax of the party was the arrival of the ushers and bridesmaids celebrating Kit and Bill Wheeler's wedding. They apparently prolonged the party well beyond dawn.

I did not have a coming out party *per se*, but seemed to have caused more trouble by having lots of odd activities. One early dawn, I returned from a party and woke up Mother and said, "Excuse me, but I thought I should tell you that I have invited thirty people for breakfast." Mother arose, set tables and at eight o'clock went to the West Street Market for oranges, eggs, Shredded Wheat and rolls. Everyone came and ate and had such a grand time that breakfast parties became the rage. I claim I was the founder of the brunch routine.

One wonderful celebration was given on Granny and Grandfather Lincoln's fiftieth wedding anniversary. The centerpiece was a marvel created by Mother out of three of the bronze statues that decorated the top of the bookcases. Venus was dressed as the bride; the Praying Boy with arms raised to heaven was robed as the priest; and Mercury in a smart cutaway was rushing to the altar, ring on forefinger.

The library statues figured prominently at many a party. The joy of teenage guests was to steal the fig leaves. One morning after a fairly sophisticated party I came down stairs to find all the statues turned to the wall!

I think the most raucous celebration I can recall was held at the beginning of World War II. Black outs were required and Mother had outdone herself. All the windows had shutters, and Mother had covered the cracks with black felt. The occasion was in honor of Submarine Commander Lincoln Marcy and Navy Ensign George McElroy. It was loud!! All the guests were sounding like various implements of war. Charlie Hamilton, returning from the night shift at the Worcester Telegram, decided not to come in. He thought the party must be over as the house was so dark and quiet. But it really was in full swing. No London blackout was more effective.

All the parties were not big and noisy. We had a few delightful dinners. While after-dinner coffee was in progress in the library one cold winter night, Mother gravitated to one register, Louisa to another and I to a third. We stood warm and comfortable as shivering guests balanced their coffee cups with numb fingers. One stranger surveyed his toasty hosts and observed, "This is the custom I've heard about." We were a little ashamed.

It was always cold in the house in spite of two enormous monsters in the cellar gobbling up coal. Thompson's successor, James Rhodenizer, used to tend them. After the fuel was changed to oil and James, as well as the Noras, Delas and Zitas had departed, Mother became the chief cook. The coal range was not used, and modern gas did not give off the same warming glow of the old stove. So Mother wore her cooking costume: a long, elderly mink cape.

After Grandfather's death in 1934, Granny Lincoln returned from the McLean's Hospital and was ensconced in the two front bedrooms with two wonderful trained nurses who each had a twelve hour shift except on Wednesdays when the night girl stayed on until noon when the day girl arrived and did the following week as a night nurse. Quite a schedule!! It usually worked well, but there was a crisis during the afternoon of the 1938 hurricane! Smoke seemed to be coming out of the fireplace in Granny's bedroom. Fire!! She had to be got downstairs. Luckily there was more than one nurse around. Mother and I held the window shutters shut against the wind. By good luck, two actors with whom I had just finished a summer stock season happened to be there and they and Uncle George and the nurse bounced Granny downstairs on a mattress. She never went back upstairs, but lived in the two parlors from which her hospital bed could have been pushed out of the long windows in the event of a disaster.

No more hurricanes disturbed her. On Granny's death 49 Elm was owned by Uncles Dan and George and Mother. Grandfather had claimed he would only put in a few repairs that would last his lifetime and eleven years after his death we were still drifting along on his repairs: ceilings crumbling; jungle growing in the beautiful garden; paint peeling. But, it was a wonderful house to live in. During World War II, Granny's upstairs suite was converted to an apartment where Aunt Emma Dresser lived. On her death, Waldo returned from the war and lived there with his wife Lou. Their oldest son, Tom, was born there. He was the last of Levi's descendants to live at 49 Elm.

In 1950, the land was sold to the Worcester Fire Insurance Company of which Levi had been the first president. The house was moved to Old Sturbridge Village, a move resulting in great part from Louisa's insistence that the house was a piece of architecture worth preserving. Mother and all her goods and chattel were moved to 65 Wachusett Street. Mother could not bear to think of leaving the house in any but spic and span condition, so I was dispatched to wash the woodwork. I was perched at the top of the library scrubbing away at the cornice when in came Mr. Wells of Sturbridge Village, a big wig from the Fire Insurance Company and a couple of engineers. They discussed the destruction of the house in order to move it to its new seat. They never noticed the gaunt cleaning woman scrubbing away at what was about to be demolished.

I felt very sad, but not as sad as Frannie did when the Junior League had a luncheon in '49' at its new address in Sturbridge and she was asked about her life in the old manse. She found it difficult because at the time the house looked more like a Howard Johnson!

RLD, standing, with Louisa and Nanny Rutherford in Somes Meadow (1914)

After a year of nursery school at Miss Albee's where her German teacher, Emilie Schiele, was reputedly deported as a suspicious alien, Rosie spent the next twelve years at the Bancroft School. Named after George Bancroft, the historian and a distant relative of Rosie, the school was located then at 93 Elm Street, a short walk down the street from 49 Elm. Rosie made some of her deepest friendships at Bancroft. They were an eclectic and talented group, most of whom lived in the neighborhood: Janet Barton Morgan (cousin, poet and the first Episcopalian female deaconess), Kay Clark Morgan (wife of an Amherst music professor), George Bullock (cousin, insurance executive and blue water sailor), Babbie Bullock Chute (cousin, professional monolinguist), Millicent Ewell Tuckerman (a leading New England horse breeder), Charlie Morgan (Amherst professor and author of books on Michelangelo and George Bellows), Liz Dewey Marangoni (expatriate in Florence with a speaking part in *Room with a View*), Amy Bess Williams (benefactor of Hancock Shaker Village) and Paul Morgan (industrialist and proprietor of the Vernon Stiles Inn, Connecticut). At Bancroft, Rosie also became actively involved in dramatics, her future profession.

Rosie's first summer on Mt. Desert was spent at Seal Harbor in 1912 where the family encamped after a number of years switching between West Chop on Martha's Vineyard, Watch Hill in Rhode Island and Nonquit on Buzzard's Bay. Two summers later, in 1914, the Dressers—largely through the urging of Aunt Nancy Greenough, a member of Ga's 1893 Sewing Circle in Boston—moved up Somes Sound to Somesville where they rented a comfortable house in Somes Meadow that looked out on the harbor and the mountains beyond. Perhaps, it was from that porch that Rosie first saw the mesmerizing "pinky glow" of early evening light reflecting off the distant mountain granite.

At the time there were no cars allowed on the island, so travel was by buckboard or boat. The family spent the better part of the summer in Somesville—hiking, rowing,

Frank Farnum Dresser—dressed for the office—rowing RLD and Louisa under the docks at Somesville (1914)

going on picnics and visiting relatives and friends who were summering elsewhere on the island. Hayrides were a great attraction. So was rowing with Frank Dresser who took to the oars with lawyerly finesse and attire. He was a good sport since he preferred cerebral pursuits—the law, reading and watercolor painting—to anything athletic. As his wife, children and fellow rusticators scampered over the mountains, Frank Dresser—a non-hiker—liked to sit on the porch where he said he, "got my exercise watching the mountains." These idyllic summers became the foundation of Rosie's lifelong love of Down East Maine, in general, and of Somesville, in particular.

As a child Rosie spent only two summers away from Mt. Desert. One was spent at Pinelands Camp on Squam Lake where her rebellious older sister, Louisa—returning for her second summer—insisted that Rosie speak to no one, an impossible command for the sociable younger sister to follow. The other was in 1923 when Rosie, age fourteen, joined her family for a Jamesian year abroad. During that year, Rosie and her elder sister traveled with their mother and, occasionally, their father, throughout the Continent. While half the family was gallivanting across Jazz Age Europe, the youngsters, Waldo and Frannie, were left with their nurse, Annie Rutherford—later Nanny Bruce—on her family's simple farm in northern Scotland for the better part of the year, an extended separation that would be frowned on today. It was during this year abroad while she was living with her family in the south of France, that Rosie heard the tragic news that her father had died unexpectedly in Worcester. Life changed quickly.

As Rosie recounts above, the Dressers had already moved into the large family house at 49 Elm Street in 1919. On Frank Dresser's death, Rosie's grandparents, Waldo Lincoln and Fanny Chandler Lincoln, gamely moved back into their child-filled house. Waldo Lincoln was an august, even forbidding, personage, but he proved to have a soft spot for his grandchildren and their friends. His wife, Fanny Chandler Lincoln, stayed with them initially, but, suffering from a degenerative mental disease, she was soon placed in the gilded seclusion of McLean's Hospital where the family visited her regularly. Rosie's mother, Ga, took over a household that at the time included three maids, a nurse, a gardener and a driver. Her father, Waldo Lincoln, paid the bills. On Waldo Lincoln's death in 1934, his wife

Fanny returned home from McLean's. As a graphic display of Fanny's presumed grief, her family sent her portrait back to the Boston painter Frederic Vinton, and asked him to darken her dress and paint out a vase of flowers in an already subdued picture he had painted of her some years earlier. The Lincolns were masters at finding oblique ways to publicly signal private sorrow.

President of her senior class and head of the student government, Rosie graduated from Bancroft in 1927 and joined her elder sister, Louisa, at Vassar. Louisa was in her third year, and was a formidable scholar, about to be elected Phi Beta Kappa as a junior. Rosie was more intrigued by the social possibilities than the academic opportunities at Vassar. She had a great time, and made many lifelong friends during her year in Poughkeepsie. During that formative year, Rosie was particularly inspired by Hallie Flanagan, the gifted head of the Vassar Experimental Theater who counted Pirandello, Stanislavsky and Lady Gregory as direct influences and friends. Flanagan later headed the Federal Theater Project and—with a cool feistiness that reminds one of Rosie—famously informed Joe Starnes, a hostile Dies Committee congressman, that Christopher Marlowe was not, in fact, a Communist but was, instead, "the greatest dramatist in the period immediately preceding Shakespeare." A seasoned presence like Flanagan must have re-enforced Rosie's theatrical ambitions. As Rosie later told a *Worcester Telegram* interviewer, "I knew I didn't want college theater . . . I wanted a professional career." Her eyes were on the New York stage. Rosie left Vassar after a year to take drama courses in Boston at the Leland Powers School of Drama, and then moved to New York and an apartment on Waverly Place in Greenwich Village.

Although the New York theater was thriving in the 1930s, there was limited demand for an actress who was not an ingénue. Rosie was too tall and formidable for that. She did get a Broadway role in Julian Thompson's *The Warrior's Husband* starring Katherine Hepburn, but it was as a Greek guardsman, hardly a springboard for a young actress. The highlight of the run for Rosie was when her breastplate fell off in the middle of a performance, and she had to improvise without drawing attention to herself. Although Rosie never lost her affection for the energy, anonymity and excitement of New York, she had to move on professionally which she did.

Despite the threat of war quickening through Europe, Rosie left for Greece where she spent the better part of 1937 and 1938 with her cousin Janet Barton Morgan and her husband, Charles Hill Morgan, Director of the American School of Classical Studies in Athens and an art historian on sabbatical from Amherst. Janet and Rosie kept an eye on the three Morgan children, and traveled throughout the country visiting ruins, going to Byzantine church services, seeing plays and cruising the Aegean. Returning from her visit to the Antioch dig in June of 1938, sister Louisa passed through Athens and reported back to their mother, "It was wonderful being met by Rosie. She doesn't look a bit fatter and . . . is having a wonderful time in Greece . . . the winter has been the greatest possible success for her." Earlier in the year, Louisa had written, "Everywhere I hear news of Rosie from those who were on the Hellas cruise with her. She was evidently the life of the party and I am continually introduced and recognized as 'Rosie's sister'." The Mediterranean was a smaller, cozier place in 1938.

That July, Rosie returned to Worcester, and was appointed Head of the Drama Department at Bancroft School, her alma mater. During the summers she was actively involved in summer stock productions, including a season out in Brookfield with the Louise Galloway Players featuring the Broadway star, Louise Galloway, and the Hollywood comedian, ZaSu Pitts, whose nasal voice was the inspiration for Olive Oyl's in the original Popeye cartoons. In 1940 and 1941, Rosie co-owned and managed the Red Barn Theater in Westboro, Massachusetts where she gave talented young actors like John Forsythe, Tom Drake, Wendell Corey and her cousin Helen Marcy early starts on long careers. She also engaged famous stars like Tallulah Bankhead whose careers were in eclipse.

"Let there be light!" said God, and there was light!
"Let there be blood!" says man, and there's a sea.

Lord Byron, *Don Juan*

chapter TWO

Rosie Dresser and the Second World War

RLD on board and off to war as a Red Cross *volunteer (1940s)*

By 1943, World War II was approaching full force, and Rosie, at thirty-four, felt left behind. She took a train down to Washington and convinced a skeptical Red Cross supervisor to accept her as a volunteer even though she had no obvious wartime skills and had no medical qualifications whatsoever. The supervisor liked Rosie's spunk, and decided that her theatrical experience qualified her to join the Red Cross as a volunteer recreation worker. Her younger sister Frannie, who was working with the Office of Strategic Services in Washington, wrote to Rosie, "Oh, you're going to be one of those people one hates and avoids on boats!" But Rosie was convinced it was the fastest way for her to get overseas and into the war. On August 13, she sailed from New York aboard the *Louis Pasteur*, a converted troopship. Traveling with occasional air support, but no convoy, they arrived a little over a week later in Liverpool.

The Red Cross—the "Great American Mother", as Rosie referred to it—gave her the choice of serving in a recreational unit assigned to a specific field hospital or in a centralized entertainment division serving the Army as a whole. Despite her theatrical training and her experience managing the Red Barn Theater, she opted for the hospital and the front lines. She was assigned to the 12th Evacuation

Hospital, initially in Redgrave Park, Suffolk, subsequently in Carmethen (Wales), then Manchester and, finally, Weymouth in the south of England.

Rosie was assigned to the hospital along with two other Red Cross volunteers as a pre-invasion experiment to see what role "recreation" could play in a military hospital. Rosie's unit was so effective that similar Red Cross units were later assigned to each of the Evacuation Hospitals following the Allied troops across Europe. In England, few of the patients Rosie initially encountered had combat injuries. The exception were crew members of the US Eighth Aircorps—a "wonderful unit of flyers", she later wrote—who had been injured in the early fighting on the continent. But most of the patients in the 12th Evacuation Hospital before it crossed the Channel were soldiers injured in driving accidents or other careless mishaps. The war in Europe remained remote.

Seemingly charmed, Rosie's social life in England was intensified by the ominous prospect of future battle. She took full advantage of the slow military build-up to make frequent visits to London for the theater and for dinner with old friends on leave like Paul Morgan, George Bullock and Waite Hurlburt. Having dinner in London with Paul Morgan, her old friend and near Worcester neighbor growing up, she later recalled, "we had so much to talk about that finally we looked around the restaurant and all the chairs were on top of the tables." She made regular visits to Welwyn Garden City to see the Putleys, an English family whose three daughters had been taken in by the Dressers at 49 Elm

Street during the Battle of Britain and who would stay with them for the better part of the war. She became close friends with kindred Red Cross volunteers like Lettie Jones. In a tea shop, Rosie met a Woodstock cousin "who had married a very rich Englishman and was quite a war worker . . . very attractive . . . she had entertained my parents when they had been in England." More eye of the storm than holiday, Rosie's first six months in England were more familiar than threatening, more of an extended family reunion than a rigorous preparation for war.

This relaxing interlude changed abruptly in the spring of 1944. The hospital was moved to what Rosie described as "a pasture in the south of England", just outside of Weymouth where she saw first-hand the steady build up of a major expeditionary force. The official history of the 12th Evacuation Hospital describes the momentous night of June 5 as follows:

> On the night of June 5-6 at about 1100 hrs, a heavy drone of aircraft was heard in the distance. Soon the white, green and red lights of the planes formed an almost unbroken line stretching from horizon to horizon, coming from the west and heading toward France. This was followed by many such formations in succession, until the sky was completely dotted with lights of the planes. We then knew the Invasion had begun.

Earlier that afternoon, Rosie and her good friend Lettie Jones had been assigned to a nearby airbase to cook supper for the men. They worked late into the night feeding exhausted crews and serving them coffee. Interviewed some years later for an oral history, Rosie described the rest of her evening on June 5, 1944:

> Suddenly the Major, or whoever was in charge, came up and said, "You girls shouldn't still be here. You've got to get out of here right away." So he got a driver, and he said to him, "Don't come back. When you get to the field hospital, stay there." It was quite late at night. We were very tired. It had been really hard work. We came back and we were the only people awake in the field hospital . . . I felt in my bones there was something in the air that was peculiar. And, in just a few minutes, the invasion started. We could see them flying over. They flew so low.

Rosie recalled being more inspired than terrified as she watched successive waves of bombers and their fighter escorts flying directly overhead in tight formation and low to the ground. She knew they were headed across the Channel to France. D-Day had begun. She was finally going to war.

Despite the awesome sweep of planes that flew across the south of England to Normandy that night, the next few days were fraught with rumor, many auguring poorly for the Allies. Rosie later wrote, "It was another day before the casualties came in. All the wounded said, 'It's a failure. The invasion is a failure!' Of course, it was to the wounded, dead and dying. But we gradually heard of its success."

Rosie spent the better part of the European war with the 12th Evacuation Hospital, following Patton and the Third Army as they battled across the continent. After landing in late July on Utah Beach, Rosie and the Hospital moved successively from bivouacs in Normandy to Bonneval,

Verdun, Nancy, Luxembourg City and, finally, Frankfurt. Although still technically a recreation worker, she pitched in—as everyone did—on the bloody business at hand. The makeshift hospitals near the front in which she worked were primarily focused on triage. They evacuated the seriously wounded but curable soldiers as quickly as they could. As a result, most of Rosie's time was spent with those left behind—soldiers with mortal wounds and little hope of survival and soldiers with minor injuries who would be returning quickly to battle. In hospitals near the front, death was a form of deliverance. It took all of Rosie's skill as an actress and strength as a person to minister to the dying while trying to bolster the shaken spirits of those healthy enough to return to battle.

Rosie was never a hero worshipper—even when it came to her ancestors—but she made an exception in the case of General George Patton. He made frequent visits to the hospital, never forgetting the sacrifices made by the injured as he pushed his healthier troops forward in the war. Rosie had the opportunity to see him on a number of his trips to the wards as he visited his men, conferred with doctors, and charged up the staff. She admired his uncommon ability to connect with the men, and his preference for visiting alone without the large, protective entourage fancied by most generals. His brusque, imperious reputation disguised a natural compassion that Rosie never forgot.

The hard-earned military success of the Third Army's campaign across Europe bears remembering. In Patton's summary letter to the "Soldiers of the Third Army, Past and

Present", he wrote:

> During the 281 days of incessant and victorious combat, your penetrations have advanced farther in less time than any other army in history. You have fought your way across 24 major rivers and innumerable lesser streams. You have liberated or conquered more than 82,000 square miles of territory, including 1,500 cities and towns, and inhabited places. Prior to the termination of active hostilities, you .had captured in battle 956,000 enemy soldiers and killed or wounded at least 500,000 others. France, Belgium, Luxemburg, Germany, Austria and Czechoslovakia bear witness to your exploits.

History of the 12th Evacuation Hospital

General Patton leaving the hospital at Nancy (1944)

It was a bloody whirlwind, and Rosie was caught up in it. She surely admired Patton's closing words: "The one honor which is mine and mine alone is that of having commanded such an incomparable group of Americans, the record of whose fortitude, audacity and valor will endure as long as history lasts."

Rosie came in for praise as well. An Army friend, Bob Reider, met a "Regimental Commander of the 26th Division . . . one of the best and finest officers I've met . . . an Army Colonel who holds just about every decoration possible . . . [who] said that Rosie was doing a magnificent job and was responsible, to a large extent for his pleasant memories of his stay at the hospital . . . that particular hospital will probably go down in the story of this war as having done one of the outstanding jobs of all the hospitals."

Rosie's war letters home are flush with affection and respect for the enlisted men, especially those gravely wounded. On February 19, 1945 she wrote about how much she was looking forward to an imminent visit to Paris "even if it is just a mess of Americans on leave." She continued, "It will undoubtedly be good to see some healthy soldiers; a steady diet of the dismembered is trying on the point of view. The most aggravating thing is that their point of view is so perfectly remarkable that it makes one ashamed to have it depress one's own outlook."

Their resilience was well documented in a striking thirteen-page photo essay published in the January 29, 1945 issue of *Life* magazine. Ralph Morse, one of the pre-eminent photojournalists of his generation and later the Senior Photographer for *Life*, tracked the step-by-step experience of a wounded Third Army soldier, George Lott, from the moment he arrived at the battalion aid station in Lorraine to his eventual rehabilitation in Elmira, New York, 4,500 miles away. Six hours and ten minutes after being wounded in action, Lott arrived for surgery at the 12th Evacuation

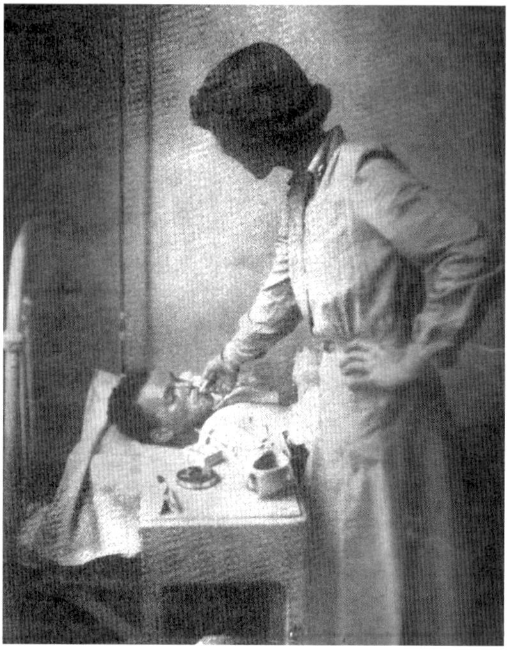

Ralph Morse/Time Life Pictures/Getty Images

Rosie tending to George Lott, a wounded soldier in the 12th Evacuation Hospital at Nancy (1945)

Hospital in Nancy where Rosie was stationed. The surgeons successfully stabilized his wounds so he could be evacuated safely to England for more thorough treatment. Rosie is photographed giving Lott a cigarette following his surgery. The caption reads, "Lott . . . showed great patience in learning to depend on others." Rosie, of course, knew that war was a matter of mutual dependence. She depended as much on the inspiration of men like Lott, as they did on her and others like her.

Although inspired by its transcendent moments, Rosie had no illusions about the savagery of war. *Life* magazine captured both dimensions, but the war movies of the 1950s that shaped so much of America's early "memory" of the war sanitized the real carnage. Whether it was the Battle of the Bulge, Iwo Jima, the deserts of North Africa or the jungles of Guadalcanal, soldiers shot in the war movies made prior to, say, *Deer Hunter* or *Apocalypse Now* appear to be hit with pacifying darts rather than flesh-tearing, limb-shearing metal. Bodies stayed intact. Death was sad but painless. In *The Boys' Crusade*, Paul Fussell quotes a German Master Sargeant who recalled the darker, more depraved side of war:

> The never ending detonations . . . burning vehicles from which piercing screams could be heard—a soldier stumbling, holding back his intestines which were oozing from his abdomen—soldiers lying in their own blood—arms and legs torn off—others driven crazy, crying, shouting, swearing, laughing hysterically.

In July of 1945, a *Worcester Telegram* reporter who interviewed Rosie wrote that, "Miss Dresser is reluctant to speak of her experiences. Obviously, she has seen much of the war at an evacuation hospital which handled operative cases." Rosie knew intimately that war was Hieronymous Bosch, not Norman Rockwell.

As they fought their way into Germany, Patton and the Third Army discovered the concentration camps. On visiting Ohrdruf, a satellite of Buchenwald and the first camp liberated by the Allies, the war-hardened General vomited at its sights and smell. At Buchenwald, Patton paraded the German townspeople through the camp to witness directly the consequences of Nazi savagery.

Rosie witnessed it herself in the death camps near Linz, Austria. Rather than return home when the 12th Evacuation Hospital had been disbanded in May following V-E day, she volunteered for the 121st Evacuation Hospital located in Linz, the *Patenstadt* or adopted hometown of Hitler. Her description years later of trying to save the prisoners was vivid. The rescue workers took barely living, emaciated bodies from small bunks and placed them in baths of water to get moisture into their desiccated systems. Most of the prisoners were unable to eat anything until this had been done, and a number did not survive. She talked about the experience some forty-five years later as she herself sensed the onset of death. But when Rosie was asked in a 1945 *Worcester Telegram* interview whether she had seen the camps first-hand, she said no. It took her four decades to talk about what she had seen.

This horrific experience, perhaps combined with Patton's own attempt to volunteer for Asia, may have inspired Rosie to transfer to the Pacific after the war in Europe was won and Germany had been defeated. In July of 1945, Rosie left for the Philippines, traveling via Worcester where she enjoyed a thirty-day leave. She arrived in Manila on August 14 soon after V-J Day, but well in time to witness the war crime trials of two notorious Japanese generals: Tomoyuki Yamashita, Supreme Commander of the Japanese Forces in the Philippines, and his subordinate, Masaharu Homma, who forced Filippino and American prisoners on the Battaan Death March. Both were convicted and executed.

Attending the trials may have given Rosie a sense of closure, because, with the war over in both the European and Pacific Theaters, she returned to Worcester rather than visit occupied Japan as she had been invited to do.

Rosie arrived home on January 8, 1946 with no plans for the future, a short lived aimlessness shared by the Italian writer Iris Origo. In response to an upbeat radio broadcast by Churchill about the battle for Anzio, Origo wrote in her war diary, "I wish I could share his feelings . . . It is odd how used one can become to uncertainty for the future, to a complete planlessness." That seems to have been Rosie's own state of mind in January 1946, nearly three years after volunteering for the war. She spent the spring and early summer relaxing with her family at 49 Elm Street. The large family house, filled as it was with eighteenth and early nineteenth century portraits, furniture and stories, must have seemed at once both alien and familiar, jarringly anachronistic and gracefully timeless.

Hard as it must have been to make sense of the experience, Rosie soon discovered a detoxifying antidote for her three intense and transformative years at war. She began looking for a house to buy in the coastal village of Somesville, her childhood *acadia* on Mt. Desert.

"Aunt Bee lifted her glasses, deliberately abandoning the subject, to scrutinize two lonely terns, riding by us on a floating crate, then gave her absorbed attention to the beauty of the silhouette of Mt. Desert island as it loomed nearer."

Helen Howe, *The Fires of Autumn*

chapter THREE

Somesville and the Island of Mt. Desert

RLD and Ga celebrating Somesville's Bi-Centennial in period costume (1965)

Somesville is located on the island of Mt. Desert at the head of Somes Sound, the only natural fiord on the East Coast. Settled in 1761 by Abraham Somes, the village has the most protected harbor on the island, and was an active commercial center for the better part of the nineteenth century. A lumber mill, a tanning factory and a shoemaker's shop were clustered near a mill pond in the center of the village adjacent to a tidal cove. There were several small boatyards as well as a small community of fishermen. Mrs. Seth Thornton's 1936 account of Somesville's founding notes that, "Somesville is a sprinkling of Neo-Greek cottages, very Palladian" suggesting that the original settlers had arrived, "equipped with a Bible and a book of Greek architecture."

Known in the early nineteenth century by the clumsy, but descriptive name Twixt-the-Hills, the village is nestled between mountains that slope down to both the east and west edges of the Sound. A mile wide just outside Somes Harbor, the Sound runs six miles down to a narrow mouth with Northeast Harbor on one side and Southwest Harbor on the other. Somesville is equidistant between the two and has straddled the two sides of the island culturally, not just geographically, for years. Never as elegant or overtly social as Northeast or Seal harbors, Somesville was not quite as quiet as the so-called "Quiet Side" of the island to the west. It danced to its own special drum.

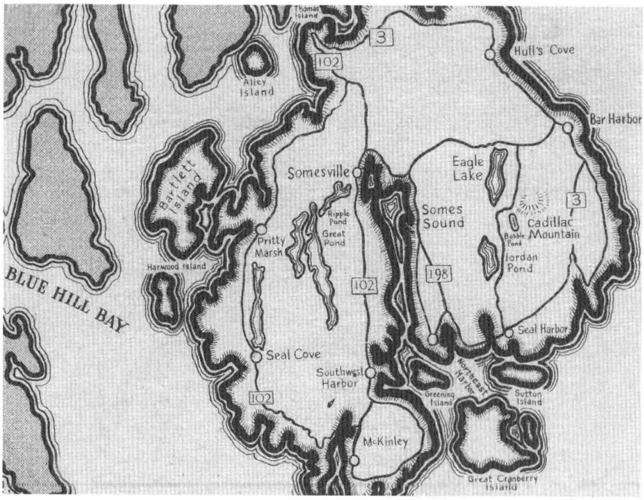

Map of Mt. Desert Island and the Cranberry Islands (1950s)

Mt. Desert began attracting summer visitors in the mid-nineteenth century. Its varied scenery and magical light appealed initially to painters like Thomas Cole, Frederic Church and Sanford Robinson Gifford who were famous for their Hudson River pictures which saturated a nascent art market in the 1850s. Mt. Desert was less accessible than the Hudson and offered rich new material for artists who found in one idyllic spot more subjects than most could handle: the ocean, tidal and occasionally ominous; mountains, some densely forested, others bald; pink granite shores and mud flats; fields, some gold with grain, many barren with rock;

RLD, hatless in center, with Louisa, Nanny Rutherford, the Davis children and their nurses resplendent in summer whites while hard-working field hands finish haying Somes Meadow (1914)

lakes, some long and oval, some short and round, virtually all set against mountains; all manner of ships, well-weathered buildings and equally weathered people. Combined with the ever-mutating weather—foggy mists, crystalline sun, luminous haze—those subjects challenged some of the finest artists of the period with a virtually infinite range of subject matter. A roster of painters—up to the present day—gives some idea: Thomas Cole, Frederic Church, Sanford Robinson Gifford, Fitzhugh Lane, Louis Comfort Tiffany, William Stanley Haseltine, Alfred Bricher, William Trost Richards, John LaFarge, John Singer Sargent, Childe Hassam, Carroll Tyson, John Marin, Oscar Bluemener, William Zorach, John Heliker, William Keinbusch and Richard Estes.

Mount Desert House—*Daniel Somes' inn visited by Frederic Church in 1855, later owned by Bishop Manning and his family (1960s)*

In order to accommodate the artists and early tourists, a small number of rooming houses sprang up. In 1855, Frederic Church and Charles Tracy—the future father-in-law of J. P. Morgan—stayed with their traveling party in Somesville at the *Mount Desert House* two doors down from *The Cobbler's* in the center of the village. In his diary, Charles Tracy described the local economy of the time: "Commerce and fisheries are the business of everybody here. A man gets a clearing, a cottage, a yoke of oxen, a cart and a sloop or schooner. They fish and coast, and build vessels."

That quaint description was quickly dated. Tourism on Mt. Desert began in earnest following the Civil War. The combination of mountains and ocean, fields and lakes proved irresistible. As the travel writer Clara Barnes Martin wrote in 1866, the summer visitor could "find in one [spot] the Isle of Shoals and [Mount] Wachusett; or Nahant and

[Mount] Monadnock; or Newport and the Catskills." By the turn of the century, tourism accounted for a major share of the island economy. Of course, the tourists then were not short-term visitors arriving in ungainly recreational vehicles or overloaded station wagons. Largely from Boston, New York and Philadelphia, they were a surprisingly fertile mix of college professors, Episcopal divines, rich industrialists and financiers—people with the time or the money, and often both, to stay for the better part of each summer. Sharply distinct summer colonies formed. Bar Harbor rivaled Newport for its grand devotion to gilded consumption. Northeast Harbor, known as "Philadelphia on the rocks", became a center of yachting and elegant shingled cottages. The Rockefellers transformed Seal Harbor into a quiet, understated village with "all the simplicity that money could buy". The Episcopalian Lawrences and other Bostonians made Southwest Harbor, on the other side of the island, a prosperous center of conspicuous under-consumption.

For all their subtle variation, the summer colonies—especially Seal Harbor, Northeast Harbor and Bar Harbor—were unified by an unusual confluence of private wealth and public interest when it came to preserving some of the island's most distinctive scenery. Industrious volunteers and philanthropic supporters initiated efforts to preserve the land and to make it more accessible by developing a trail network linking the mountains and the villages. Their efforts were both prescient and successful. Beginning with the creation in 1901 of the Hancock County Trustees of Reservations, their signal achievement became a national park that evolved from Sieur de Monts National Monument in 1916 to Lafayette National Park in 1919 and, ultimately, to Acadia National Park in 1929. The creation of the 35,000-acre park—much of it donated by John D. Rockefeller, Jr.—effectively saved the island as a natural wonder. Although summer residents failed in 1915 to keep Mt. Desert free of cars and failed again two years later to prevent a bridge from being built to the mainland, they ultimately succeeded—with the active support of the local

Somesville from the air with The Cobbler's *to the far left and the Somes House left of center (1950s)*

community—in preserving over a quarter of the entire island as a national park.

Somesville, perhaps due to its central location between each of these summer communities, attracted families that wanted the best of several worlds. They wanted the peacefulness of a small nineteenth century village on a quiet harbor, one famously painted by Fitzhugh Lane in 1850 that had changed little since then. But they also wanted easy access—on their own terms—to friends, relatives and sporting facilities in the social enclaves nearby. Some families gravitated towards Northeast, some towards Seal, some towards Southwest and a few towards Bar Harbor. Somesville, though, was the real center of gravity. Except for its short-lived yacht club, the town never had—and never needed—its own tennis, swimming or sailing club. The Somes House and its dock, the Post Office and the general store were the social magnets in Somesville, especially in the 1950s. Each gave year-round and summer residents —lobstermen and scholars, plumbers and industrialists, carpenters and novelists—a common ground, a natural chance to rub shoulders, put a face to a name, confirm a prejudice or, as likely, debunk one.

Rosie had the good fortune to buy *The Cobbler's* just as the village was entering a golden phase. The war was over. The national economy was about to rebound. The Old Guard—local and summer—was still in evidence, but was refreshed by new faces. Some newcomers—like Rosie —had long standing connections to Mt. Desert while others brought entirely fresh eyes. Traffic was still light. People used the old names for the mountains—Robinson, Dog, Brown, Eastern Western, Western Western—rather than those invented by the Park Service—Acadia, St. Sauveur, Norumbega, Mansell, Bernard. Motorless schooners drifted into Somes Harbor with the help of tides. A farmer used a horse rather than a tractor to rake Rosie's field behind *The Cobbler's*. High tea was common. So were picnics to the outer islands and long hikes on empty trails. There were no fiberglass boats. In the summer, Franklin stoves and primitive electric heaters with glowing orange coils took the edge off icy morning air. Wooden boats were still being built—one or two a summer—in a small boat shop in the center of the village. Lobstermen used heavy wooden traps. Croquet was more popular than golf. Telephone calls were made on party lines using heavy, black phones with stiff rotary dials. During the summer, a flower-man visited *The Cobbler's* every week with a large basket of freshly cut flowers for sale. The Somes House, just across the street from Rosie, served Sunday lunch in a large, austere dining room that looked out on freshly mowed fields sloping down on three sides to the harbor. The tablecloths were like parchment, stiffly starched and brilliantly white. At night, the village of Somesville was very quiet, something that made the occasional sound of a distant motor or a foghorn unnerving.

Of course, the real charm of Somesville was the community itself, summer and local. Rosie crossed more social lines than most, but the social lines in Somesville were, for the most part, softly drawn. The thirty members of the Woman's Literary Club of Mt. Desert, a Somesville organization, included published summer authors like Helen Howe and Margaret Ayer Barnes as well as six other summer residents. The Mt. Desert Yacht Club, a shorter lived Somesville organization, was run by summer residents but welcomed local sailors and kept its yearly dues low—$10 for a family, $5 for an individual—to make membership accessible to all. Of course, buying and maintaining a boat was another matter.

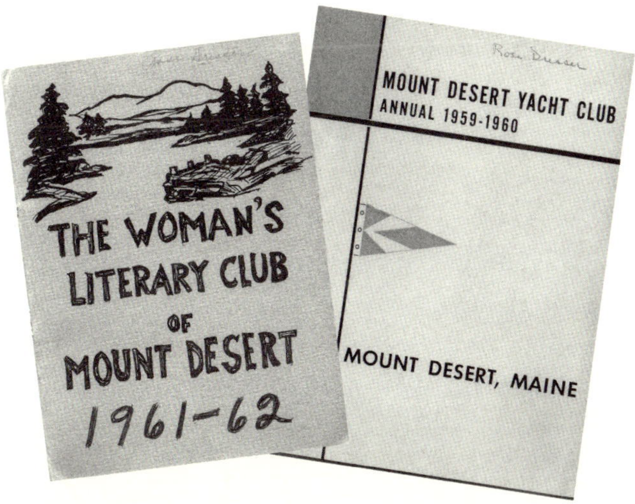

Yearbooks of the Woman's Literary Club of Mt. Desert and the Mt. Desert Yacht Club—the former still thriving, the latter long gone

It would be overly romantic to claim that Somesville was a large, happy and extended family. It was a refreshingly eclectic mix of people—fishermen, inheritors, writers, storekeepers, undertakers, architects, industrialists, carpenters, ministers, caretakers, boat builders, teachers, naturalists —who, at the least, tolerated each other and often seemed to genuinely enjoy each other's company. Somesville residents —summer and winter—who meant much to Rosie in the 1950s included: Margaret Barnes, the Pulitzer Prize winning novelist, and her husband, Cecil, a Chicago lawyer and their three sons Edward, Bunny and Cecil—respectively, an architect, a surgeon and an engineer; John Fernald, the carpenter who restored *The Cobbler's*; Bob and Norma Fernald, shopkeepers; Arthur Bunker, the harbormaster; George Mikhalapov, a very white Russian, and his irrepressible wife Anne Biddle; Agnes Grant, a talented cook; June Smith, the postmaster, and his wife, Julia; the leading Episcopalian of his day, Bishop William Manning of New York, his wife, Florence, and their daughter, Frances; Bob Patterson, an architect, landscape designer and civic leader and his wife Barbara, a naturalist; Helen Howe, an author, and her husband Reggie Allen, the first general manager of Lincoln Center. People and place made Somesville home for Rosie.

But once again, we are skipping ahead of the story. The 1950s in Somesville—and afterwards—were special for Rosie, because during two industrious months in the summer of 1947 she was able to transform *The Cobbler's* from a tired shell of a building into a gracefully rejuvenated summer house in the center of the village. As described in the letters that follow, her hands-on restoration of *The Cobbler's* became something of a community project, one that captured the imagination of a cross-section of Somesville residents—summer and local, older and younger, ancient friend and new acquaintance. Although Rosie could not have guessed it at the time, the summer she spent in Somesville restoring *The Cobbler's* in 1947 became the social and emotional foundation of the rest of her life.

The Cobbler's *from the backfield shortly before the barn fell and long before the trees grew out (1947)*

"The whirlwind has passed and now,
whatever destruction it may have left,
we can begin to build again."

Iris Origo, *War in Val D'Orcia: An Italian War Diary*

chapter FOUR

Restoration Summer

RLD sweeping out the back entry hall of The Cobbler's *(1947)*

1947 was a pivotal post-war year. Combatants were distancing themselves from the trauma they had seen and survived. Some moved from war to political restoration—the Marshall Plan designed to rebuild Germany as a democratic state was announced that year, and the Occupation in Japan was simultaneously laying similar groundwork to rebuild that country, also in an American image. Although the post-war economic boom was slow to emerge, the technological foundations were set in December of 1947 when John Bardeen and Walter Brattain collaborated with William Shockley to develop the transistor at Bell Labs. Key elements of post-war American hegemony were emerging while Rosie was looking for, buying and restoring her small house in the village of Somesville.

Anecdotally, one can reasonably assume that immediately after the war active combatants who had risked their lives in battle were likely to make different career and life choices than staffers who had spent the war on safer ground well behind the terrifying front lines. After the armistice, staff people were still well equipped to think in terms of bold, "big picture" projects, and the post-war world is doubtless better off as a result. But the frontline fighters—infantry-men, tail gunners, torpedo specialists, medics—especially those who had barely escaped or witnessed too much death were naturally inclined to think in narrower, more domestic terms. For many, the concrete fact of surviving the war overwhelmed the abstract glory of winning it. Marriages and birth rates spiked upwards. So did new housing starts. Many returning from war wanted to forget their immediate past—the haunting images, smells and sounds of war—and focus on lawns, entry-level jobs and resurrecting their lives. Rosie was one of those.

Interestingly, there is not a word about the war in the fourteen letters that Rosie sent from Somesville to Worcester between June 23 and August 1, 1947 describing her life in Somesville and her progress in restoring *The Cobbler's*. There is no hint of it, not even as a distant backdrop. Of course, that is not to say the war had no impact on her. It was a life defining experience. But the effects were powerfully sublimated and deeply disguised in good Yankee fashion.

In reading these letters and in knowing Rosie, it is hard to sense her outsize personality. At times, she seems almost demur and anxious not to draw too much attention to herself. Although she has the independence, rare in women of that period, to be out on her own physically restoring a house, she makes light of it. It is an adventure not a crusade, a project not a mission. And she has a refreshing openness to people from backgrounds radically different from her own pre-war life. That independence and newly found openness *might* be attributable to her war experiences. Ministering to injured men from all walks of life on the edge of battle must have affected her deeply—democratizing her and promoting a *carpe diem* sensibility. But the war itself is not even remotely apparent in these letters. There is no mention of it, no allusion, no trace of it, even between the many lines. The three years Rosie spent following Patton across a Boschian Europe appear to have vanished from or, at the very least, retreated deeply into her psyche as she restored *The Cobbler's* during the summer of 1947.

What is apparent in these letters is Rosie's drive to restore something—in this case a house—and her pleasure in the seemingly tiny moments of community life that enriched her summer. It is not surprising that she chose to return to Somesville, a village that had been such a happy part of her childhood—a time of hayrides, long climbs, a nurturing Nanny, a benevolent mother and a devoted father who died while Rosie was in Europe at the age of fourteen. In Somesville, time seemed to have stopped while the rest of the world was abuzz with change. Except for the arrival of cars on the island in 1915 and the opening of a bridge connecting the island to the mainland two years later, Somesville was still the quiet, harbor-side village Rosie remembered as a child. A psychologist might infer some regressive attraction. If so, it was a self-protective and healthy response to unspeakable war experiences. One thing, though, is clear: the summer of 1947 was profoundly restorative.

Preface to the Fourteen Letters

Rosie's forceful personality is subdued in these letters. That gives the anecdotes center stage, but makes it harder for the reader to get a good fix on her. As a person she was formidable, crisp, direct, hyper-energetic, extroverted and entirely unreflective. She commanded attention when she walked into a room. Part of it was her theatrical bearing, part of it was a natural self-confidence hammered into her from an early age. She could be Hepburnesque—wry, composed

Part Katharine Hepburn: RLD as Lady Bracknell in Oscar Wilde's The Importance of Being Earnest, *Foothills Theater Company, Worcester (1982)*

and elegant; but she also had a broad streak of Lucille Ball —loud, physically dominant, playful. Not surprisingly, she was often cast or, rather, type-cast in particular roles: as Lady Bracknell in *The Importance of Being Earnest*—including a 1950 performance at the Casino Carousel in Bar Harbor—or the Empress Dowager in *Anastasia*. But she also loved playing in home-grown spoofs such as *The Three Scrooges*, a rhymed skit she wrote and performed with her two sisters at the family Christmas Eve party in 1962.

Part Lucille Ball: RLD teaching her great-nephew Sam Truesdell how to drink from a bottle while celebrating her 75th birthday at The Oaks, *home of her Paine ancestors (1984)*

Despite her theatrical style, surprisingly little of Rosie's large persona is evident in these letters. As she herself wrote home on Independence Day in 1947, "I try not to be any more of a character than I can help." Like so many others returning from the frontlines of war, she was simply trying to find a small, secure place in the world—somewhere she

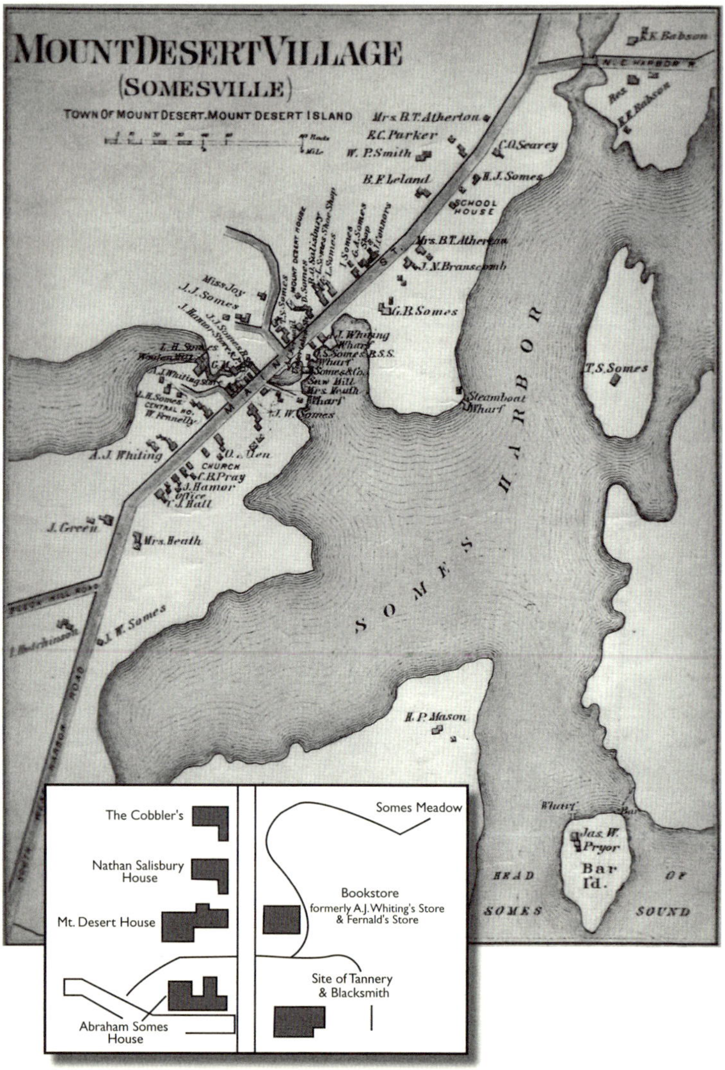

Historic Somesville showing The Cobbler's *(L. Somes), Sheep Island, (T.S. Somes) and the Somes House (G.B. Somes) with detailed inset of the village*

could call home after three years in tents, troopships and make-shift housing.

On a summer holiday in 1946, Rosie had begun looking in Somesville for a house to buy with the support of Louisa who had agreed to cover most of the expense. Rosie was traveling with her mother who sent a post card home on August 10 reporting, "So far we have made no progress. Having a grand time." Later that month, Rosie's younger sister Frannie, on holiday from Yale, discovered that the Lewis Somes house on Somesville's main street was for sale. Rosie moved quickly, and on November 10, 1946 she and her two sisters, Louisa and Frannie, bought the house from the J. Lowell Grindle family for $5,000. Rosie's uncle, Daniel Waldo Lincoln, advised that her Bar Harbor attorney should be sure to see the property first hand to "make sure the description is approximately correct. I do not say exactly because these country titles are very difficult, but apparently you are buying a house with a two and a half acre lot, more or less."

Three decades later, in 1975, the Somesville Historic District was established, and eight houses in it were formally entered on the National Register of Historic Places. *The Cobbler's* was one of them. The citation noted, "The chaste lines and double gabled façade make this dwelling a pleasing element of the Village landscape." That may have been true in 1852 when the house was built, and it certainly was true in 1975 when the citation was written. But in 1946 the house would have been better described as a "promising wreck". Both the barn and the cupola above it were tottering. One of the floors inside the house had a large hole that opened onto a cellar with a dirt floor. Plaster was falling from the walls, and the plumbing did not work. The front porch was falling down. The house had not been painted for years, inside or out. Rosie would have been forgiven if she had chosen to tear the house down rather than restore it. But that never seems to have crossed her mind. Despite its wobbly barn, its shaky walls, and its dangerous floors—*The Cobbler's* had strong roots in Somesville's past. Fresh from the wasteland of war, Rosie was not about to sever them.

Daniel Somes, builder of *The Cobbler's*, and his brother Lewis, the subsequent owner, were grandsons of Abraham Somes who had founded Somesville in 1761. Daniel operated a tanning factory on Somes Cove that supplied leather to a shoemaking shop that Lewis and his son, Lewis, Jr., ran for many years. In 1831, Daniel left the tanning business when he inherited a house on the main street of the village that soon became "the first public house" on Mt. Desert. Daniel made a successful transition from tanner to taverner by converting his inheritance into *The Mount Desert House*, a nineteenth century Bed & Breakfast catering to early summer "rusticators" and artists such as the Tracys and Frederic Church. In 1852, Daniel built a new house on a lot across the street from Somes Cove directly adjacent to *The Mount Desert House*. This is the building that Rosie bought and restored ninety-five years later. She named the house *The Cobbler's* because Daniel later gave it to his shoemaker brother Lewis who lived in the house for many years and whose shop was nearby.

THE LETTERS

The fourteen letters Rosie wrote home during the summer of 1947 describe in some detail how she restored the house. They serve here as the basis for a narrative that approaches the summer as a story organized around the correspondence. Each letter is introduced with additional background on some of the people, institutions, situations and events. This is the "plugged" version. As mentioned earlier, the reader may choose to simply read the letters themselves, unedited and un-amplified—the so-called "unplugged" version. They are included here *verbatim.*

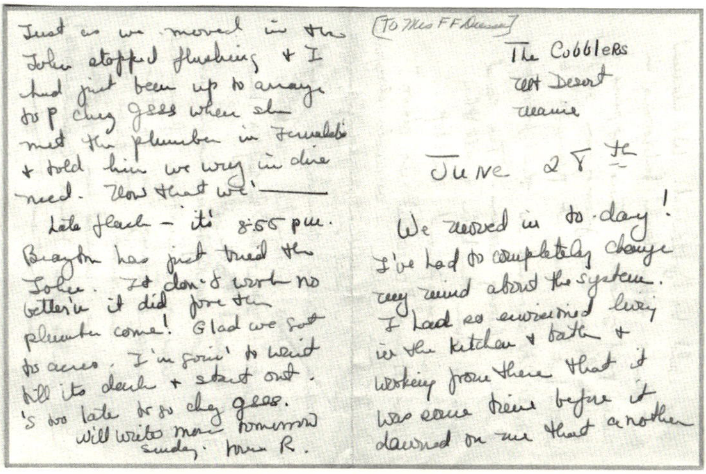

[To Mrs F F [illegible]]

The Cobblers
Mt Desert
Maine

June 28th

We moved in to-day! I've had to completely change my mind about the system. I had so envisioned living in the kitchen & bath & working from there that it was some time before it dawned on me that another

Just as we moved in the John stopped flushing & I had just been up to arrange to [illegible] when she met the plumber in [illegible] & told him we were in dire need. Now that we'——

Late flash – it's 8:55 pm. Brayton has just tried the John. It don't work no better'n it did fore the plumber come! Glad we got [illegible]. I'm goin' to wait till its dark & start out. 's too late to [illegible]. Will write more tomorrow Sunday. Mom R.

Facsimile of RLD's letter home June 28, 1947

The cupola at The Cobbler's *shortly before it fell into the barn (1947)*

Day One/Letter 1: June 23, 1947
"Brayton's theory about making good time is to keep going + not to race."

Having purchased the house on November 10 the previous year, Rosie made her inaugural trip to *The Cobbler's* eight months later on June 23, 1947. Departing from Worcester at six-thirty in the morning with her first cousin, Brayton Lincoln, Rosie arrived in Somesville at four in the afternoon after a nine-and-a-half hour drive. They had taken country roads from Worcester to New Hampshire since neither Route 128 nor the Massachusetts Turnpike was yet open. In Maine, they drove most of the way on Route 1, long before it was choked up with tourists and shops. This was the first of several hundred drives that Rosie, the new homeowner, was to make over the next forty-three years between Somesville and her future residences in Cambridge, Worcester and Woodstock, Connecticut.

Rosie was more accustomed to the leisurely trips to Mt. Desert she had enjoyed as a child on long summer holidays taken with her family in the early twentieth century. At Union Station in Worcester, the Dressers would board the *Bar Harbor Express*, a summer train that originated in Philadelphia. The *Express* connected them to a steamship that took them from Boston to Rockland where they would board the *J.T. Morse* for the overnight leg to Northeast Harbor which was the most memorable part of the trip. Passengers marked the beginning of their summer holiday when—on being awakened for an early breakfast—they came out on deck as the *J. T. Morse* was entering Blue Hill Bay and the sweeping hills of Mt. Desert—the "elephants" as the Dressers called them—were coming into panoramic view. After arriving in Northeast Harbor, the Dressers would be met by a boatman who would ferry them up the Sound on the short and final leg of the trip to Somesville.

Fellow travelers: RLD with her scholarly sister Louisa (mid 1950s)

The automobile and the opportunity to make a living changed all that. Years later, when Rosie was teaching at the

Winsor School in Boston, she would dash down to Somesville on fall weekends—"12 hours of driving for 36 hours of bliss," she said. Her elder sister, the scholarly Louisa, made those quick weekend jaunts more complicated. One Friday afternoon in the 1950s they met up in Boston for the drive downeast. Louisa told Rosie she had one quick errand—she needed to drop an overdue article in the mail for *Art in America*. Anxious to beat the rush hour traffic, Rosie double-parked outside the downtown Boston Post Office as her sister went in to mail her manuscript. Constitutionally impatient, Rosie waited. And waited. And she waited. Finally, she parked the car, and stormed into the Post Office where she found her elder sister standing over a narrow desk finishing her article in long hand using a ballpoint pen attached to the desk with a short metal wire. A scholar's work is never done. The rest of the trip was made in silence and lots of rush hour traffic.

Soon thereafter, Louisa's brother Waldo offered to drive her to Somesville in their Willys wagon with his wife, Lou, and their three children, Tom, George and Richard. She accepted with the caveat that she needed to stop for a moment at the Farnsworth Museum in Rockland. Waldo was agreeable and some four hours into the trip they pulled into Rockland. Louisa disappeared into the museum, and Waldo or Lou went off in search of ice cream cones for their three young boys. An hour later, Louisa had not yet returned. The ice cream long gone and with the boys getting restless, Waldo went into the museum to look for his time-blind sister. Much to his surprise, he found her in a large gallery lecturing to a rapt audience about early Maine paintings. Virtually every family trip downeast, especially those prior to the opening of the Maine Turnpike, became the basis for lively, involved and endlessly repeated stories.

One drive almost ended tragically. As reported by the *Ellsworth American* in 1984:

> Police said a Woodstock, Connecticut woman escaped serious injury August 12 when her car left the road on Route 1 and rolled over. Police said Rose L. Dresser of Woodstock fell asleep at the wheel of her 1983 Subaru which swerved across the road and hit a signpost. As the driver awakened, the car was skidding across the road where it rolled over in the travel lanes on Route 1.

Rosie made light of this unnerving tale. She delighted in the fact that her only injury occurred when a helpful state trooper released her seatbelt and—hanging upside down like a bat in her over-turned car—she strained her shoulder falling back to earth. Sheepishly, she later confessed that an extra glass of lunchtime wine visiting a friend in Blue Hill on an already long drive from Boston was the likely culprit.

Thirty-seven years earlier in 1947, Rosie and Brayton made stops in Portland, New Castle and Ellsworth before arriving in Somesville late in the afternoon on "a beautiful day". They picked up the key to the house, and bought groceries across the street at A.C. Fernald's, the general store on the tidal cove diagonally across the street from *The Cobbler's*.

Over the next thirty years, Fernald's became a cornerstone of Rosie's life in Somesville. In the summer, the store carried fine canned goods from S.S. Pierce, exotic teas and crackers and superior meat, well butchered by Mr. Grant who tossed the entrails into the shallow cove behind the store. Far more appealing to Rosie's nephews and nieces, Fernald's also sold candy cigarettes—especially the killer brands Pall Mall, Chesterfield, Lucky Strike and Camel. Every summer Rosie included a pack or two as pillow presents for her young visitors, socializing the children into the adult world at cocktail hour when they learned to take leisurely drags on candy cigarettes while sipping Shirley Temples. Many years later in the 1980s, Rosie and her neighbors tried to buy the empty A.C. Fernald store to use as a boathouse, but the Fernald family wanted an exorbitant amount for the building despite the fact that it had virtually no land and no plumbing. It has a much higher and far better use today, not as Rosie's boathouse, but as one of the better bookstores on the Maine coast, the aptly named Port-in-a-Storm.

On arriving in Somesville, Rosie and Brayton got right to work. They "put on working clothes" and inspected the house. Their first impressions must have been unsettling, even bleak. Rosie conceded that "a cursory glance revealed much junk in the cellar + shed . . . no evidence of the mental or physical efforts of J.F. and practically no barn left." Things looked grim to Brayton, a recent graduate of Kenyon College who would live with his young family in Havana briefly during the 1950s and later become the town manager of Hull, Massachusetts. In retirement, he would write a history of the plastic screw. Rosie quickly overcame any initial apprehension and boldly concluded, "it all looks wonderful", a feeling confirmed when she and Brayton met early that evening with "J.F." John Fernald was a master carpenter, a sometime employee at the family store and the person who deserves the fullest credit for transforming *The Cobbler's* from a wreck into a tiny jewel of a house during the summer of 1947. Rosie described their "reception" from John as "wonderful" and their conversation as follows:

> After 15 minutes of hearing how all he had to do at the store + all he had to do shingling other roofs + how ill he had been all winter bit by bit it came out he has talked with a painter, investigated the shed problem, found a mason + plans to remove the porch himself. He arrives at dawn tomorrow to git down to brass tacks. We will have only a discussion he says. He is in wonderful form.

Rosie and Brayton later dressed for dinner in Southwest Harbor and took "a turn on beach + cemetery" before calling it a very long day. They had taken rooms with Georgia Somes Smith Stanley, "G.S.S.S." in Rosie's letters, just down the street. Georgia Stanley was a remarkable woman. A descendant of Somesville's founder Abraham Somes, she ran a dry goods shop, served as postmistress for Somesville and operated a rooming house. A day later Rosie reported that Mrs. Stanley was "nuts for Brayton" but had a "setback" when she was cleaning what she thought was his bedroom and came across "cold cream, hand lotion, red polish + toilet water" on the bureau. She told Rosie, "That young man takes good care of his skin!" Mrs. Stanley was delighted when Rosie told her that the room she had been cleaning was hers, not Brayton's.

The Cobbler's *as RLD and Brayton saw it on Day One (1947)*

Mon June 23

To whom it may concern:

After a prompt start at 6:30 we drove along in good time. Brayton's theory about making good time is to keep going + not to race. It proved successful. We had 3 brief stops:

Soda at Portland
Gas at New Castle
Lunch at Ellsworth

We drove on to Mt Desert at 4. It was a beautiful day and a good time in it to arrive. We picked up key & groceries at AC Fernald's + settled ourselves in our rooms. Put on working clothes + unpacked car, no small job! We put all stuff in future living room + took stock. A cursory glance revealed much junk in the cellar + shed, lots of stuff left by Smiths + no evidence of the mental or physical efforts of J.F.

There is practically no barn left! We took a walk over the premises + Brayton made his first comment: "Here is a good place to pitch a tent." But I think it all looks wonderful. We then went to call on J.F. It was a wonderful reception. It did my heart good. After 15 minutes of hearing how all he had to do at the store + all he had to do shingling other roofs + how ill he had been all winter bit by bit it all came out that he has talked with a painter, investigated the shed problem, found a mason + plans to remove the porch himself. He arrives at dawn tomorrow to git down to brass tacks. We will have only a discussion he says. He is in wonderful form.

Then we got dressed + went to Southwest Harbor for dinner. Then called on Mrs Harry Somes. The Morris family was out so have no news for WLD's till tomorrow. But the trip was worth it for the juicy bits. Took a turn on beach + cemetery and then went to bed where I am now.

Much love

R.

Day Two/Letter 2: June 24, 1947

"We really did pretty good with the paper peelin'. There were seven layers in the little bed room. Each one more hideous than the last."

At nine the next morning, Rosie and Brayton met again with John Fernald who said "he ain't even a'goin to talk about estimates" because—as he wisely observed—"we ain't Rawkerfellas." That was certainly true, although Rosie had been relieved the day before when Burton Fernald "refused cash for the groceries + said yr credit's good round heah." John outlined his plan of attack: take down the shed and the barn; install a hot water heater in the cellar; get a plumber to put in a wash basin; take off the front porch; open up the fireplace. Rosie did not get the impression that any of this was going to happen quickly, but observed that John "sure is in a good mood. Still wishes he'd bought the house himself."

Later that morning, Mrs. Stanley "carried pots of boiling water to us . . . on her last trip she brought a fruit knife with her + said she was of a mind to give us an afternoon's labor. And she did. She peeled paper like a veteran fur 2 hours! Gawd bless her." In describing their progress Rosie wrote at the end of the day, "We really did a pretty good job with the paper peelin'. There were seven layers on the little bedroom. Each one more hideous than the last. When we scraped off the last layer, half of one wall fell in so we've got to do a mite of plasterin . . . where the ell joins the main house."

Taking a short break from the paper peeling, Brayton fiddled with an old organ in the back of the house and was delighted to find that it still worked. A long day came to a productive end.

John Fernald supervising the demolition of the front porch (1947)

Tuesday June 24th

Dear all –

To-day was another perfect day. G.S.S.S. called us at 7 + after a special breakfast (prepared by me – Ha! Ha!) we got to work. A steady dose from 8-6. Time out at 11:thirty to eat two delicious Harriet ham sandwiches, lettuce, tomatoes, milk + veg juice (prepared by me Ha! Ha!) and another breather at 3 – a coke. The ha has are really on me because now that summer is here G.S.S.S. says she really can't feed us because the S-House + the Homestead are very jealous if she serves meals since she ain't got no license. And she depends on them for roomers. But she is a little lenient about offering us everything + her kitchen privileges are nothing like Block Island's! We went to Bar Harbor for dinner to-night + had a real "do" at Testa's Restaurant.

But enough of this - You want to know about the house.

First, Brayton is magnificent! He is the hardest worker I ever saw + very competent. G.S.S.S. is nuts over him and whistles her admiration steadily. I'm afraid she'll wear out her dentures over him. She suffered a slight set back this morning when she was doin' up our rooms. She was making my bed + thought she was in his room. She spied cold cream, hand lotion, red polish and toilet water ranged along the bureau.

"My land" she said to herself, "that young man takes good care of his skin!" She was relieved to discover that her idol was not quite so effete.

John came over 'bout 9. He ain't a goin to even talk about estimates. But we had quite a chat about the fact the we ain't Rawkerfellas. (Was relieved to have Burton refuse cash for the groceries + say, "yr credit's good round heah.")

John says he's a mind to separate the barn + jack up the shed but he don't know when he'll get to it. If he can't find a fella he'll supervise him. The remains of the barn will drag down the shed + the shed will drag down the house + we might as well have stayed in Worcester if he don't. But he's a mind to save the barn so we can think about it.

He has got a fella to put in an electric water heater in the cellar + put in a fire box big enough to carry the wood. He says he gisses it won't pauperize us + he'll let me know jist as soon as he can what it'll be. He's got a plumber to put in the wash basin. "Taint done yet but he's plannin' on it."

He didn't get to the well last fall. He can't do it now cause there's so durn much water there at present. He sez if we keep our minds on not bein' so clean it'll carry us thru till fall which is good well-diggin time. But what water we'll git will be hot.

John's a gonna take off the porch himself right away. (That may be bout September at the current rate of attack.) But he sure is in a good mood. Still wishes he'd bought the house himself.

He's got a mason to open up the fireplace but I don't know just when that feller'll get around here.

When John arrived he come with a step ladder so now Brayton + I each have one. G.S.S.S. carried pots of boiling water to us in the morning. On her last trip she brought a fruit knife with her + said she was of a mind to give us an afternoon's labor. And she did. She peeled paper like a veteran fur 2 hours! Gawd bless her.

We really accomplished quite a lot on our first day. The first thing we did was to carry all the junk the Smiths had left all over the house out to the shed to wait for the junk man. I never would have made it without Brayton! Then we started to peel the paper off the little down stairs bed room. Brayton stayed at it all a.m. + it's a tough job. I took an hour out to talk with John.

Then Bridgam Fernald popped over. I thought he had come to give us the glad hand. GSSS thought he had come over to argue over the boundary but what he really had on his mind was to say he had all the old carpets from the house stored away in kerosene + didn't we want to buy them. Of course he's so deaf he doesn't yet know whether I said yes or no. But the whole time he was a tradin' John kept a yellin' at me nawt to buy. I didn't. In the midst of all that Miss Frances Darling of the Bay Colony Book Shop came to call. She too is deaf as a hen. I ain't got a lung left after all that. And the little that remains is filled with plaster so it don't amount to much.

GSSS has a new expression:

"There's everything in the fruit closet but gold."

"There's everything in the cellar but gold."

"There's everything in the bureau except gold."

But she can't apply it to the scenery. There sure is gold in them thar hills. They *are* so lovely. And what's more we can see 'em pretty good from jest about every window – except the back south ones + we got Bridgam there. Perhaps we can see them carpets.

We really did pretty good with the paper peelin'. There were seven layers on the little bedroom. Each one more hideous than the last. When we scraped off the last layer half of one wall fell in so we've go to do a mite of plasterin. Have to show it to John in the mornin'. I hope it ain't much of a job. It's the side where the ell joins the main house so I think that's why it happened.

We got that room all scraped + started on the kitchen. Got that about 1/3 done.

I don't know if you will consider these assets or not but we have inherited 2 cats. The Smiths left them behind June 7. When their legs began to look like Ethel Fernald's she threw them a fish bone. GSSS sent them some milk in a saucer to-day. I ain't bein' too hospitable to 'em but I don't know as I can harden my heart much further. And every time I look at the rat possibilities + the shed + the barn me heart gits a mite softer.

Brayton has found that the organ works + wants to fix it up so I giss we won't give it to no junk man.

That about brings you up to date on things.

Love

Rosie

Brayton feeding a new member of the family (1947)

Day Four/Letter 3: June 27, 1947
"The Electrician...discovered a mite o' pipe trouble. I asked if I would have to marry a millionaire . . . He laughed s'hard he durn near fell into the cesspool."

On June 27, Rosie updated her family on the progress made over the past three days. The electrician had turned on the power and a new electric heater had been ordered for $252. A plumber spent time in the cellar looking for a spot to place the heater and "discovered a mite o' pipe trouble." Rosie asked him if she "would have to marry a millionaire to pay for that" and the plumber "laughed s'hard he durn near fell into the cesspool + said 'You got that idea at the right age. I had it thirty years too late'."

The following day, Rosie would announce in triumph to her mother, "We moved in to-day!" Doing so took some risky improvisation. They "cleaned out the 2 upper back bedrooms in main part of house. There happens to be a hole in the floor of one so that is the kitchen since it permits 6 cords to descend to the floor plug in the living room. The card table is over the hole + all the electrical equipment is on top . . . sounds dangerous as hell." Brayton shaved using water heated by dropping an electrical coil into a basin of water and turning the switch. It is amazing the house survived its saviors.

West and East: the length and breadth of The Cobbler's *(1947)*

June 27

TBD
Lou + Thos -

So very sorry you can't come. But will see you soon.

Waldo -

Will be looking for you after the 4th. Have arranged with GSSS for you to stay here, $2.00 a night. You can kitchen privilege at the Cobblers + get dinner at the Homestead. Dying to see you. So glad you're coming!

Lou D, Frannie + JRD, mere

The Electrician arrived yesterday + turned on the power. The Plumber arrived to-day. The electric heater is ordered $252.00. More for his services. When I tried to find out what they would be, he said "Don't know, can't tell. John says you ain't Rockefeller." He then went down cellar + looked at place for heater. Discovered a mite o' pipe trouble. I asked if I would have to marry a millionaire to pay for that. He laughed s'hard he durn near fell into the cesspool + said "You got that idea at the right age. I had it thirty years too late." was s'flattered I durn near fell into the cess pool.

The painter comes to-morrow for a chat. I hope it's not such an expensive one.

The mason who is going to fix the open fire place ain't a goin' to come till fall. He says fire places is winter work. He's up to Farmington now gittin' 12.00 dollars a day. John says he'll do it mighty cheap this fall. But I guess we won't have any heat this year. So glad I brought them andirons. John promises to take off the porch Monday. But at his rate that may be a fall job too. But he's mighty impressed with the am't of work we've done to date. All paper – peeling and cleaning. But progress is coming. John says to get all the peeling done then he'll get a plasterer for ½ a day to fix all bad places "cheaper for you than gittin' him several times."

Much love

R.

Restoration well underway (1947)

Day Five/Letter 4: June 28, 1947

"GSSS was sorry to see us go . . . she's enjoyed being 'in' on this unique restoration."

Seemingly on the fly, Rosie sent a quick but memorable note marking the day that they actually moved into *The Cobbler's*. The house, for the most part, was not ready. As noted earlier, a hole in the floor of an upstairs bedroom allowed Rosie and Brayton to connect six electrical cords with an outlet in the living room. The jury-rigged electricity appeared to work even though it was "dangerous as hell". The same could not be said of the plumbing. Despite the earlier ministrations of a plumber, it did not work. Ever resourceful, Rosie planned to "wait till its dark + start out". Three years living in tents across Europe had prepared her well for her first weeks living in *The Cobbler's.*

[To Mrs FF Dresser]

JUNE 28th

We moved in to-day! I've had to completely change my mind about the system. I had so envisioned living in the kitchen + bath + working from there that it was some time before it dawned on me that another plan could be followed. We cleaned out the 2 upper back bedrooms in main part of house. There happens to be a hole in the floor of one so that is the kitchen since it permits 6 cords to descend to the floor plug in the living room. The card table is over the hole + all the electrical equipment on top – Mrs Haines "carried us down" a unique affair – sounds dangerous as hell. You plug it in, pop it in a basin of water, turn on the switch + in a few minutes you have hot water! It works!!! Brayton has just shaved with it.

GSSS was sorry to see us go, for other reasons as well as financial. She's enjoyed being "in" on this unique renovation. To ease things up a bit we "carried her up" an old double bed frame (unbelievable!) She took on somethin' though just as we moved in the John stopped flushing + I had just been up to arrange to p chez GSSS when she met the plumber in Fernald's + told him we were in dire need. Now that we – late flash – it's 8:55 pm. Brayton has just tried the John. It don't work no better'n it did fore the plumber come! I'm goin' to wait till its dark + start out. It's too late to go chez GSSS.

Will write more tomorrow Sunday.

Love R.

A handcrafted Christmas card from Georgia Somes Smith Stanley (1947)

Day Six/Letters 5 and 6: June 30, 1947

"Mr. Hinckley's an awful good worker but John says . . .
'you never know when he's goin' to go off on a drunk.'
Financially my picture is bleak."

On June 30, Rosie wrote to her family at 49 Elm, "June goes out on a great deal of progress + . . . today was the most constructive of all". They had completely cleaned the shed and the barn—"it's a big job + the least attractive AND ITS DONE!!!"—and "John + Mr. Hinckley knocked off the front porch", the removal of which "caused quite a stir in the neighborhood + brought in a lot of callers."

Rosie's letter home on the thirtieth also describes a Gothic incident worthy of Faulkner, Stephen King or Harry Crews. Cleaning out the attic, Rosie found "Lew Somes' dentures. Upper + lowers both! I give 'em to John + he give 'em to Mr. Hinckley cause he don't have any. I found that out when I give him a caramel this morning." Although it may seem primitive to a contemporary reader, John Fernald's generous intervention was more practical than morbid. Maine in 1947 was poor. Dentures—whether retrieved from the attic of a dead man or newly pressed in a dental laboratory—were a valuable item. Resourcefulness was then, and remains today, a characteristic coastal virtue.

Of course, it was not all work in the state that eleven

Brayton Lincoln, mop in hand, at the back door (1947)

years earlier had begun embossing "Vacationland" on its license plates. The Gilpins, friends of Rosie's mother, generously made a sailboat available to Brayton for the weekly yacht club races. The Mt. Desert Yacht Club had a relatively short lifespan, in part because of the curious choice of boats —Hustlers, centerboard cat boats with long booms—and in part because Somesville was not an especially "clubby" place. Serious racers could join the Northeast Harbor Fleet, and serious cruisers simply gunkholed along the coast. But during the 1950s, the local club flourished, and Brayton was an early beneficiary of it. Races were held on Sunday and Wednesday afternoons. On race days both Somes Harbor and the head of the Sound were speckled with darting white sails and enlivened by the occasional shot of a signal cannon. The Gilpins, who lent Brayton their boat, were—along with another Philadelphia family, the Disstons—among the earliest summer rusticators in Somesville. Both families were friends of Rosie's mother, Ga, dating back to the Dresser's Somesville summers some forty years earlier.

Waldo Dresser and Brayton Lincoln rigging the Gilpins' dinghy (1947)

Never much of a sailor, Rosie was particularly pleased to discover that Brayton had literary as well as nautical interests. "Brayton delights my soul in a thousand ways" she wrote, "but the thousand and oneth was that he is laughing out loud over *Pride and Predjudice*."

Rosie was disturbed to learn on the thirtieth that her near neighbor, Miss Frances Manning, had "persuaded Dr. Grindle to let her go thru the stuff in the house and . . . put several things in the 'museum'." Rosie wrote in *faux* anger, "I could strangle her." Frances Manning was the unmarried daughter of the eminent Episcopal Bishop of New York, William T. Manning. Episcopalianism was at its highest tide following the war, and Bishop Manning was at its apex. Miss Manning lived with her parents during the summer in the storied *Mount Desert House*, which was two doors down from *The Cobbler's* on the main street of the village. As noted earlier, Charles Tracy and Frederic Church had stayed there in 1855 when the house was a tavern and rooming house run by the entrepreneurial Daniel Somes.

In the Manning era, *Mount Desert House* was the site of lively cocktail parties. One memorable evening, bats flew into the back of the house, and the Bishop and his wife grabbed tennis rackets and stood on chairs to swat them. The Bishop was five-foot two inches. His daughter, Miss Manning, was a physically more commanding presence who later inherited *Mount Desert House* where she lived year round for the better part of the rest of her life.

Concerned about the accumulating expense of restoring *The Cobbler's*, Rosie wrote a separate letter on the thirtieth to Louisa, her elder sister and patron backer. Rosie described her current financial predicament as "bleak". She was just back from the war and the family had scraped through the Depression in a large mansion house that was expensive to maintain. Louisa had a good job as the curator of the Worcester Art Museum, but Rosie was unemployed and money was tight. This letter—focused as it is on the cost of gasoline and the fact that Brayton "requires a full meal a day"—shows how careful Rosie was with every cent she spent. This tightness continued after she received her share of several family inheritances that eventually lightened the pressure on her. Even with money in the bank, Rosie always felt "broke".

June 30th

Dear All

June goes out on a great deal of progress + quite a head-way has been made.

To-day was the most constructive of all. The shed + barn was cleaned out! It took one 2 ½ ton truck filled, and Kelley's small truck made 4 trips creaking in every joint. It's a big job + the least attractive AND ITS DONE!!!

This afternoon John + Mr. Hinckley knocked off the front porch. The house is really going to be sweet. In cleaning out the barn we found the blinds for the door: good!! We will have to put on a step or two as there's a four foot drop now. A bit awkward.

The removal of the porch caused quite a stir in the neighborhood + brought in a lot of callers. Mrs John Fernald appeared. Also Mrs. Bob + baby. 2 complete strangers dropped in + Miss Mannin' come over in all her glory. I discovered from her that she persuaded Dr. Grindle to let her go thru the stuff in the house + she put several things in the "museum". I could strangle her – but I'm sure the Smith children would have destroyed them so perhaps it's just as well. Mrs. Haines tells me the Lew Somes cobblers bench is in the Islesford Museum. Wish we could get hold of it. Curator Dresser or Secretary to the Head of Yale had better try. I will stick to the manual labor.

Peter Bunker has dropped in a couple of times. I *love* him. He thinks he knows of a row boat we can rent. He told the Gilpins Brayton was interested in sailing + they have offered him one of their boats to race while he is here. Mrs. Gilpin tells me we should take out a membership ($10.00) in the Yacht Club + then Dressers can sail on one of their boats. The Gilpins are sweet. Mr. G. had a stroke last winter + can hardly talk. We went to see them this eve to discuss the boat + Brayton is going to change his profession from house peeling to boat painting + help Mr. G. fix a boat for the race on Sat.

I saw Nancy Greenough for a breathless buck-toothed moment. So you see I'm on wheezing terms with them rusticators every now + again.

Speaking of teeth – What do you think I found in the attic! Lew Somes' dentures. Uppers + lowers both! I give 'em to John + he give 'em to Mr. Hinckley cause he don't have any. I found that out when I give him a caramel this mornin'.

Mr. Hinckley's an awful good worker but John says when he gits a holt of him he works him hard all day cause you never know when he's goin' to go off on a drunk. John says Miss Mannin' takes a skin ful now + again too and gits powerful ugly when she does.

Brayton delights my soul in a thousand ways but the thousand and oneth was that he is laughing out loud over Pride + Prejudice.

It's most ten-thirty. I must git to be. We start our day at six but that's about an hour + a half later than some other folks. We've got about a 1/3 of the living room left to peel + that finishes the downstairs wall peeling. John has a plasterer who will come in + do the bad plaster work + then we'll patch it up + start paintin' the downstairs. The painter comes over for a chat about the outside. He's a goin' to think over the situation. John suggests painting front + side toward Parker's + littin' the Fernald side go till next year. Sounds sensible. What do you think?

Much love,
Rosie

The front porch comes off The Cobbler's *(1947)*

June 30th

Dear Louisa

Financially my picture is bleak. Brayton actually costs a lot in food as he really requires a full meal a day. Until today, we have had to eat in either Bar Harbor or Ellsworth + the season prices are high. Gasoline + food for the car + us has been to date 36.00 + Mrs Stanley charged 20.00 for housing two of us for 5 days. 2 bucks a night which is ½ her regular price which was nice of her but still high. We moved in here the 28th but I still have to feed Brayton. He more than earns it. He works every minute + I never would be so advanced without him. This is all leading up to the fact that I need to go in to the money that I have in the Savings Bank. Can you inquire at bank about my book + transfer 100 dollars to my checking account?

I had to write a check to Mr. Kelley for cleaning out trash + dumping same + $2.00 cash for boys at dump.

To-day we were able to start eating dinners at Homestead which is cheaper. I wouldn't eat a full meal myself but I couldn't have Brayton eat + me not. Besides I get hungry!

Please advise

Love

R.

Day Ten/Letter 7: July 4, 1947

". . . 'do you want this old milk bottle?' 'Christ yes' shouted John thru the evening air. 'That belongs to my woman here + she'll lose a nickel if I don't give it back to her.'"

Rosie and Brayton celebrated Independence Day by "sleeping until 7!!!", and then launching into the messy challenge of painting the ceilings. Their only break was "time out to bicycle up to Harry Grindle's to buy an ice box . . . a mighty rotten one . . . for which I paid 10 dollars." The food they had been trying to keep cool down in the basement had been going rancid causing both of them "a mite o' dysentery".

Although barely a week into the project, Rosie's hands-on restoration of *The Cobbler's* was beginning to get some attention in the village. She reported that Bishop Manning "hops over now + again with celestial encouragement" and "when he blessed me this morning he told me that my title in the village is now Public Beneficiary No. 1." Margaret Ayer Barnes, a Pulitzer winning novelist, "offered her son as a free architect when he arrives." Her unsuspecting son, Edward Larrabee Barnes, had just graduated from the Harvard Graduate School of Design. He was about to embark on an eminently successful career that gracefully fused elegant modernism with the vernacular simplicity found in a mid-nineteenth century house on coastal Maine. Over the years, he and his wife Mary became particularly close friends of Rosie's as did Ed's brother, Bunny, whose daughters all attended the Winsor School where Rosie taught for more than two decades.

Margaret Ayer Barnes also became a close friend of the family, especially of Rosie's mother. Her husband, Cecil, was a distinguished Chicago lawyer. On a European trip in the 1920s, Mrs. Barnes had been in a car accident that left her hospitalized for several months. In order to pass the time, she wrote *Years of Grace*, a novel that won the Pulitzer Prize in 1931. She was a theatrical figure with a solid stage presence, especially when moving around the small rooms of *The Cobbler's*. She smoked cigarettes in a chain, but never seemed to inhale. Her animated, throaty voice could be captivating to a child, even one who did not have a clue what she was saying. Her heavy horn rim glasses gave her an owlish gravity that was softened by a ready smile and a sharp wit. She died in 1967.

In a civic gesture that would have entertaining ramifications several weeks later, another new friend of Rosie's, Bob Fernald—a proprietor of Fernald's store—took the initiative to tell the Bishop's daughter, "It's a durn shame that old tree of yours + Mrs. Somes cuts off the Dresser's view of Sargent", the most majestic of the mountains on Mt. Desert. He was referring to an ungainly Linden tree that branched widely from its short trunk just across the street from *The Cobbler's* on the edge of Somes Cove. Apparently, it straddled the Somes-Manning property line. Miss Manning agreed to remove the tree, but Mrs. Somes was less accommodating. She owned the Somes House, a sprawling and perfectly sited nineteenth century inn, just across the street from *The Cobbler's* on the other side of the cove from Fernald's store. Although the tree in question was nowhere near the Somes House, the intransigence of Mrs. Somes was not unexpected. Nonetheless, Rosie was delighted that the question had been raised, and she held out hope that "we may get the pinky glow on Sargent from the front windows yet."

Rosie was also getting into the Somesville social swirl. "The Mannings invited us over Wed eve. A très gai soirée with Mrs. Greenough, Mrs. Kurtz, a miss somebody else + we all (except the Bish) had rye high balls." On the Fourth, Rosie invited John and Polly Fernald and Georgia and Ernest Stanley for cocktails to see the progress being made restoring *The Cobbler's*. Unfortunately, Mr. Stanley was captaining a launch party to Baker's Island and Mrs. Fernald was cooking for another family that day, so "Brayton and I had cocktails by ourselves", although the Stanleys were able to drop by for a brief visit at 8 in the evening. Rosie observed, "It's a little difficult to entertain when your guests ain't rusticators. Earnin' a dollar cuts into the social life somethin' fierce."

Rosie and John Fernald had developed a good, if idiosyncratic, working rapport. Vaguely reminiscent of Lyndon Johnson and Doris Kearns, "Practically all our conversations take place with him sitting on the John + me on the tub." Supplementing his carpentry, John was actively involved in his family's two principal businesses, the grocery store and the funeral home. Mrs. Stanley complained to Rosie, "that prices at Fernald's are mighty high. "Great Heavens," said she "You pay'em all your money to git food to stay alive + then they rob you soon your dead. It costs 125 dollars for a coffin now-a-days. Them Fernalds have got you comin' and goin'." Rosie loved the final line, and used it frequently over the years. But she also had great affection for the two Fernalds she knew best, Bob and John. Compared with the Somes family, the Fernalds were relative newcomers to Somesville, arriving in the latter nineteenth century from Sutton Island at the mouth of the Sound where they had an undertaking business. In a short period of time, they became the leading merchants in Somesville and doubtless the envy of some.

Both Bob and John Fernald took great delight in teasing Rosie who complained,

> I can't go near Fernald's store without getting a lot of back talk about matrimony. The other day when I was buying breakfast supplies the place was crowded + Bob was very hectic. When he was making out the slip he said what's the name. I really thought he was hectic + tired so I said simply "Rose Dresser". "Still Dresser?" he shouted "Ya bin here over a week. Haven't you changed it yet ?" Mrs. Stanley tells me that when I get this house fixed it will look so nice surely some man will want to move in!! A life of single blessedness certainly doesn't go over big around here.

Rosie concluded her July 4 letter by plaintively asserting, "I know Louisa won't believe it but I haven't been sitting on a cookie barrel in Fernald's. I try not to be any more of a character than I can help."

Independence Day

Dear All,

We celebrated the holiday by sleeping until 7!!! We didn't git to breakfast till 8!! We have begun the ceilings. It took most of the morning to sort out the paint + discover which was the one to use, I hope I chose the right one. It took me most of the p.m. to paint the 1st ceiling!! I took time out to bicycle up to Harry Grindle's to buy an ice box. He has a mighty rotten one for which I paid 10 dollars. I spent the evening scrubbin' it out. It will be fine (I hope). It's been s'durn hort everythin's bin a sourin' on me. Brayton is kinda sick o' sour milk in his coffee + the butter's been a bit rancid. So I guess 'twas an essential investment. Harry's goin' to fill it with ice to-morrow. We've both had a mite o' dysentery lately + I figure it's on account of the food goin' bad down cellar-way where I been keepin' it. They've been a robbin' us up at the Homestead for our dinners but Mrs. Morris is a mighty fine cook. The evenings there have paid dividends due to the arrival of a family named Montaigne who possess a charming daughter of 17 + a son a little younger. I been trying to line Brayton up Beech Cliff for several evenings without success. The night the M's appeared B said as we left, "Let's invite those two kids to walk up B. Cliff." They accepted with alacrity + B asked them to go sailing the next day. When I cautioned him about taking good care of them + being sure they were good swimmers B said "well if Florence can't swim + we tip over I'll have the pleasure of holding her up in the water." Attention au Romance! The Montaigne's came to call on us to-night on B's urging. I thought that perhaps our slum conditions would nip romance in the bud, but it seems the M's are interested in old homes + gave me more advice than a Rockefeller could follow. We have had a lot of callers lately. The Bishop hops over now + again with celestial encouragement. When he blessed me this morning he told me that my title in the village is now "Public Beneficiary No. I". The whole world seems fascinated by our progress. Margaret Ayer Barnes and her husband popped in + offered her son as a free architect for the Barn when he arrives. But by that time the Barn will probably have collapsed. When the Bishop's daughter was doing her marketing yesterday, Bob Fernald said to her, 'It's a durn shame that old tree of yours + Mrs. Somes cuts off the Dresser's view of Sargent. You two wommin should hack it down. So she popped in to say she would hack down her half if Mrs. S. would oblige with the other. She then went to discuss the matter with her co-owner. I saw her + a rather gloomy looking Al Hastings out looking at the tree this pm but I don't know the results. I suspect they may not be favorable or she would have told me. But I'm keeping my fingers crossed. We may get the pinky glow on Sargent from the front windows yet. The Mannings invited us over Wed eve. A très gai soireé with Mrs. Greenough, Mrs.Kurtz, a miss somebody else + we all (except the Bish) had rye high balls.

I entertained myself to-day. I lured John into taking down the porch so speedily by saying we'd have a roof raising party when it came off. So I invited Mrs + Mrs J. Fernald + Mr + Mrs Stanley to come for cocktails to-day. Unfortunately, Mrs. Fernald cooks for the Leavitts + they were dining just at that time. Mr. Stanley captains a launch for a family at N.E. Harbor + he had to take them to Baker's Island on a picnic. So the result was Brayton + I had a cocktail by ourselves. It's a little difficult to entertain when your guests ain't rusticators. Earnin' a dollar cuts into the social life somethin' fierce. However, Mr and Mrs Stanley came over at 8 p.m. when he got back from Baker's so nothing daunted we gave them a cocktail after dinner!! John came over in the middle of the p.m. to say they couldn't come. He went right into the bathroom + started rearranging the W.C. while he was explaining about cocktails. He always does that because it always needs rearranging. Someday he'll probably find me in there. Practically all our conversations take place with him sitting on the John + me on the tub. To-day we had quite a social hour because it was a holiday. Among other things he broke the news that he has two funerals since he started working on this house. I said "Heaven's John there won't be anybody left on the island if they die at this rate." "Oh yes there will" said he "I seen in the paper this mornin' that 615 babies was born in the Bangor area. We're getting' new busniz all the time." Speaking of his business, GSSS told me that prices at Fernald's are mighty high. "Great Heavens", said she "You pay 'em all your money to git food to stay alive + then they rob you soon your dead. It costs 125 dollars for a coffin now-a-days. Them Fernalds have got you comin' and goin'."

To get down to brass tacks I don't know where Waldo could call me but I guess Mrs. Ernest Stanley. She is the nearest telephone. I'll find out her number. She is on a party line. She could take the message. Since Waldo will be sleeping there she will know all about it. She still thinks Lou is coming too.

By the way please advise if you want me to apply for a telephone on this house. The Smith's had a party line of 6. We could probably get it if you want to.

Has Louisa been able to do anything about my money? I'm a gettin' nervous. I have 100 in the 5 Cents Savings Bank + at least 200 in the Worc County Trust for Savings. Would someone be good enough to forward my June statement.

Speaking of money I think John really understands I

have none. On Wednesday John spent the whole day in a hot gravel pit digging stuff for the cellar floor. Mr Hibbard was ferrying the stuff to the cellar where the littlest Kelley was spreading it out. When Hibbard was going back on one trip I sent John a orange + a milk bottle full of cold water to keep him alive so he could finish the house. When the day was over the man from whom John had borrowed the truck came to claim it. He said "Ya left some stuff in heah – here's a chain, here's a jacket and do you want this old milk bottle?" "Christ yes" shouted John thru the evening air "That belongs to my woman here + she'll lose a nickel if I don't give it back to her!"

Of course I can't go near Fernald's store without getting a lot of back talk about matrimony. The other day when I was buying breakfast supplies the place was crowded + Bob was very hectic.When he was making out the slip he said what's the name. I really thought he was hectic + tired so I said simply "Rose Dresser". "Still Dresser" he shouted "ya bin here over a week. Haven't you changed it yet?" GSSS tells me that when I get this house fixed it will look so nice surely some man will want to move in!! A life of single blessedness certainly doesn't go over big around here.

I know Louisa won't believe it but I haven't been sitting on a cookie barrel in Fernald's. I try not to be any more of a character than I can help.

Love Rosie

Day Fourteen/Letter 8: July 8, 1947

". . that girl o' his—she's an odd stick . . .
She even wants to finish high school."

On the eighth, Rosie was delighted to report home that her younger brother Waldo had arrived to join Brayton on the volunteer work crew. Waldo had served with distinction in the Coast Guard during World War II both in Europe and the Pacific. He had been a coxswain on an 83-foot Coast Guard rescue cutter that saved forty-seven drowning US and Allied soldiers during the Normandy invasion. In addition to Normandy, he saw action in North Africa, Sicily, Salerno and, later, Okinawa. Rosie and he had managed to *rendez-vous* several times in Europe during the war and had both volunteered to continue serving in the Pacific once the war in Europe had been won.

As with Rosie, the war was a defining experience for Waldo. Soon after his father's early death in 1924, he had been sent away to school, first to Fessenden and then to Exeter, in order to liberate him from the matriarchal household at 49 Elm with its three sisters, a mother, a nurse, three maids, a kind but dottering grandmother and a grandfather devoted to antiquarian research. In the spring of 1939, Waldo dropped out of Harvard—two months shy of graduation—to see the country and push beyond the cloistered world in which he had grown up. A lifelong lover of sailing and the sea, he enlisted in the Coast Guard, and quickly found himself in a *very* uncloistered world, the world of war. By all accounts, he thrived in it. So much so, he never bothered returning to Cambridge to finish his degree.

After the war, Waldo spent his career at the Norton Company in Worcester as a cost analyst. He continued to sail, was a dedicated amateur thespian and, with his wife Lou, raised three children—Tom, George and Richard—in what was then rural Jefferson, Massachusetts. In playful but observant contrast to the Herron children, Ga referred to Tom, George and Richard as the "three good boys". Every Election Day, Waldo—a Calvin Coolidge Republican—and his wife Lou—a Wellesley College "Red"—drove to the polls and cancelled each other's vote.

Although Waldo was a willing and hard worker, Rosie's account of his and Brayton's schedule shifts from scraping plaster at *The Cobbler's* to cocktail parties at the Mannings reciprocated by the Dressers, late afternoon sails on the Gilpin's boat and racing on Sunday and Wednesday afternoon with the Mt. Desert Yacht Club fleet followed by tea. Unfortunately for Rosie, Brayton and Waldo had to leave for Worcester at the end of the week. Disappointed, she acknowledged that "the reconstruction will certainly take a slump with their departure."

In her letter home, Rosie recounted two conversations with John Fernald, one somewhat disturbing, the other gratifying. In discussing a niece of his who lived in Portland, he complained, "All she does is stick her nose in a book +

read about Caesar + Cleopatra. A lot of useless trash I call it. She even wants to finish high school!" That must have grated on Rosie who had already taught young women at Bancroft and would later dedicate the better part of her professional life to them at the Winsor School in Boston. But John redeemed himself when he said that the sanding done on the woodwork in *The Cobbler's* by Rosie and her amateur crew was "smooth as a smelt". Rosie admitted that, "Not being nautical. I don't know if that means 'she' is done right or not. Maybe a smelt is scaly! But, we're carrying on as if the smelt is smooth."

Rosie refers to "pulling a Peterkin" when she describes her concern that Mr. Stanley, the plumber, and John Fernald might simply leave a "hump in the parlor floor" rather than shortening the legs of her new but oversized boiler down in the cellar. The eccentric and eponymous fictional family in Lucretia Hale's classic, *The Peterkin Papers*, seemed to remind the Dressers and Lincolns of themselves. The Peterkins were always on the verge of making ridiculous decisions. Should they cut a hole in the second floor to accommodate a large Christmas tree on the first floor? Should they open the back door to let out snow blowing in through the front door? Each conundrum was solved at the last moment by the sagacious "lady from Philadelphia" who divined the obvious: shorten the Christmas tree rather than cut a hole in the ceiling; close the front door to keep the snow from blowing into the house. Louisa played "the Lady from Philadelphia" in Rosie's life, and Rosie appreciatively acknowledged it. But none of the Dressers or Lincolns was ever comfortable crediting a Philadelphian with more common sense than a New Englander.

Waldo Dresser, volunteer house painter (1947)

July 8

Dear Dressers –

B + I were just going to bed on Sun when we heard a voice say "How do you get in?" And lo – it was Waldo. It was wonderful to see him. He, like Brayton, has worked like a dog since being here. He + B took a short sail Mon p.m. + in eve Miss Manning invited the 3 of us to her house. To-night we returned the compliment by inviting her here for a cocktail before dinner. Then we three went to the movies.

I have just written a check for $10 to the Mt. Desert Yacht Club which is a thriving organization of little boats. B. has been racing one of Mr. Gilpin's. I think he + W will race again tomorrow. They have races every Sun and Wed. with Tea afterwards. It is all ages – all kinds of boats + a very up + coming little club. The 1st tea was at Mrs. Barry Smith's. The $10 is a family membership which enables any Dressers or guests to partake of the activities.

B + W say they must return Fri. I shall be desolate. They plan to drive down to-gether which is nice for both. The reconstruction will certainly take a slump with their departure. It's hard to remember what I have told you + what I haven't. I don't think I told you John's opinion of his niece, June's daughter. The other day (when he was as usual on his namesake) I asked where he was. He said "He's in Portland doin' something with a race track." "But I've seen his family here, haven't I?" said I. "Yes" he said "and that girl o' his – she's an odd stick. She don't do anything worthwhile. All she does is stick her nose in a book + read about Caesar + Cleopatra. A lot of useless trash I call it. She even wants to finish high school!"

The other day when I was at the store Mr F asked how things were progressing. "Pretty good" said I. "When'll she be done?" said he. "August 1st I hope' said I. "I giss nawt" said he "but perhaps if John sticks to it he can git her ready for a fall weddin'! Do y'think he otter?" I sometimes think the smartest way to finish the house would be to announce a wedding date for July 28. I'll bet the Fernalds would get it ready!

Yesterday the Plumber, Mr Stanley appeared. "Has the boiler come yet?" asked I. "No" said he "but here's the bill for it". "Take it away" said I. He did but he came back again to discuss things with John. Hearing trouble I followed them into the cellar. It seems that the boiler is 76 inches tall + the cellar is 72 inches tall. Fearing that they might pull a Peterkin + we would have a hump in the parlor floor I entered the conversation. I felt I was quite an important voice but they evidently did not even know I was in the cellar. Pretty soon I heard Stanley say "Well John, the best thing to do is to dig down 2 ft + lay an entire cement floor. While your at it y'might cement the walls too." "Christ no", said John "she won't do that – at least nawt till she grabs on to that millionaire". I don't know what they decided because they didn't tell me. But I looked in the cellar later + Mr. Hibbard was laying only a small box of cement. I don't know if they plan to amputate a bit of boiler or not.

I called John in to survey our sanding of the woodwork + see if we were doing it right. He surveyed it, stroked it + said "She's as smooth as a smelt." Not being nautical I don't know if that means "she" is done right or not. May be a smelt is scaley! But we're carrying on as if a smelt was smooth.

Much love

Rosie

Day Nineteen/Letter 9: July 13, 1947

"Mr Stanley (my love, the plumber) disconnected my John Fri noon + then went away for the weekend! Glad there are a lot of trees."

Rosie sent a short update on the thirteenth reporting that an electrician was prepared to install two base plugs in each room and a hall light for $130. John Fernald had finished the front steps, and he and Mr. Hibbard had cleaned out the well. In compensating for the loss of Brayton and Waldo, Rosie wrote, "I have been getting to work at 5:30 + not laying off until after 6. I'm trying to make the day's work look as though more than I was working."

She closed with a note of gentle exasperation. "Some of the people around here are not noted for their efficiency. Mr. Stanley (my love, the plumber) disconnected my John Fri noon + then went away for the weekend! Glad there are a lot of trees."

July 13

Dear Co-owners –

The electrician was here Fri with a terrible tale. I asked him to give me an estimate on 2 base plugs for each room + a hall light. He did. $130. He has to do some work connecting up the boiler which will be additional. What do you both say to that? I asked him to hold off until I heard from you.

We could cut it down with fewer base plugs. They are $7.00 apiece. Please advise. (This does not include lights in upper ell + shed.)

Progress is slow but things are coming. John has built a set of front steps + he + Hibbard cleaned out the well. Things are more accessible + much purer as a result.

Since the boys left I have been getting to work at 5:30 + not laying off until after 6. I'm trying to make the day's work look as though more than I was working.

Let me know what to arrange with Mr. Ober. We have to have several rooms lighted. John advises doing it all now. Also, how about a stove? I found a 2nd hand coal job for $20 which I did not get. By the time it is trucked from SW Harbor it would be quite expensive. The ice box works fine. We ought to have a little electric stove.

Some of the people around are not noted for their efficiency. Mr Stanley (my love, the plumber) disconnected my John Fri noon + then went away for the weekend! Glad there are a lot of trees.

Love in haste,

R.

Day Twenty-One/Letter 10: July 15, 1947

"John Parker, the fire chief, popped in this morning + . . . produced in his filthy hand two delicious fillets of sole. At the Ritz they would have cost a buck fifty each."

Rosie's work was constantly and, no doubt, thankfully interrupted by well meaning visitors. On July 15, she reported that her mother's friends, Dr. and Mrs. Walter Seelye of Worcester and Little Cranberry Island had come by for a visit. So had Dr. Jay Grindle and his wife. Following in the footsteps of his father, Robert, who was the leading doctor in Somesville for a generation, Dr. Jay Grindle practiced for many years in nearby Northeast Harbor. Rosie was delighted to report that her plumber, Mr. Stanley, had given her a plumb so she had "arrived socially with the most valuable crowd on the island." This was soon re-enforced when:

> John Parker, the fire chief, popped in this morning + said "Have a piece of fried flounder." He then produced in his filthy hand two delicious fillets of sole wrapped up in a paper towel. At the Ritz they would have cost a buck fifty each. We sat down for a boney chew + a slight jaw during which he told me about a summer visitor who was in a store in Ellsworth yesterday. While there a rather odd man, the village drunk, shuffled in, bought something + shuffled out. The S.V. [summer visitor] said to the storekeeper, "A lot of odd looking characters aren't there?" "Yes", he said "There are – for about 4 months and then they leave."

Later that evening, Burton Fernald teased Rosie when she dropped in to buy some oranges and milk at the store. As she remembered the conversation:

> I said to Burton "You look tired", "Christ I am" said he 'what with people buying food + dying I have an awful long day. How about you comin' over + giving us a hand some night or would you be frightened to work on a body?" I gulped + allowed I'd be glad to give them a hand. He said, "Good. Bodies can't do ya no harm. It's the live ones that are bothersome."

Somesville was rich with colorful storytellers. It was also rich with generous neighbors. On July 14, Rosie and Miss Manning had visited an antiques dealer who was selling a cobbler's bench. Rosie explained that Lewis Somes' original bench was in the Islesford Museum on Little Cranberry Island. The dealer responded by offering his bench for $120, but that was too high a price for Rosie. The next day "a wonderful cortege appeared. Jenny Grindle and Miss Manning bearing a wonderful cobbler's bench." It had belonged to Lewis Somes and was painted lavender, the same color as the entire inside of the house according to his niece, Mrs. Stanley, who had dropped in to see what the fuss was about. Rosie was, "speechless with gratitude". Fifty-seven years later, that bench—stripped down to its natural wood finish—remains a centerpiece in the back shed room at *The Cobbler's*.

So is the "wonderful dry sink in the shed which", Rosie wrote, "will be a beautiful bar." She noted John Fernald's surprise when he heard the plan, asking incredulously,

"Christ, can you afford to fill all that with bottles!?" Rosie may not have been a "Rawkerfella" but her answer to John was a resounding "yes".

Frances Manning and Jenny Grindle delivering the perfect housewarming present, a cobbler's bench for The Cobbler's *(1947)*

John could be curmudgeonly. He railed about John Ames, a Somesville summer resident and distinguished Boston architect, "Christ, he's goofy." Unfamiliar with John Fernald's questionable reservations about John Ames, Rosie's future brother-in-law, John Herron, would soon join the Ames firm—Ames, Childs and Graves—after graduating from the Yale School of Architecture. He remembers Ames as a kindly Francophile who gave the office a holiday every Bastille Day. As an architectural aside, when John Herron began coming to Somesville in the 1950s, he was delighted to find that two houses in Somesville had been designed and cleverly sited by his former professor George Howe: the Thomas house at the head of the Sound and a smaller cottage at the head of the harbor that Howe had quickly sketched on a cocktail napkin for its builder, Rosie's Aunt Ruth Greenough.

Continuing to complain, John Fernald also pronounced "the Gilpin girl . . . goofy, but I always sorta liked her." Describing the rest of the conversation, Rosie wrote:

> He laughed + said "Guess you'll begin to think I think everybody's goofy – even you." But then he softened the blow by saying he would "carry down" an open Franklin fire to use in the "parlor". It belonged to "old Kate" + he had 2 + only used 1 + since it was a gift to him + he has a law with himself that he never sells a present [so] this would have to be a gift + not a sale to me.

Ga in the front parlor near the Franklin stove John Fernald gave to The Cobbler's *(early 1950s)*

The gentle curmudgeon had a lacerating tongue but a generous spirit. John Fernald's Franklin stove still warms the front parlor of *The Cobbler's* today, and, like the cobbler's bench from Miss Manning and Jenny Grindle, is a practical reminder of how considerate and welcoming Somesville residents were to Rosie during that summer and for many summers to come.

Mt Desert
Maine
July 15

Dear Family –

I am way in arrears in keeping you up to date. Since the boys left I have been on such a tight schedule that I drop asleep before I can clutch a pen.

There have been a good many callers. Did I tell you Miss Smith + Miss Cobb came last week. On Sunday Dr + Mrs Seelye appeared + later Dr + Mrs. Grindle. The 1st two calls were normal + very pleasant. The last was hysterical. To begin with, as you may recall, Grindle has a nervous affliction about the left eye which results in constant weeping which causes repeated wiping with a large dirty handkerchief + he keeps twitching the left side of his face. It got me so jittery that when I saw a tear before he felt it I would twitch my face in a friendly effort to remove his tear. I think I even got Mrs. Grindle confused. Our conversation was very odd. He would say "Why don't you shingle the rest of the roof?" I would say "why didn't you?" and so on about all the fundamentals of the house. However we parted very good friends.

Next to John my greatest love is Mr. Stanley, the plumber. He has a round stomach, a round chuckle + a round face with a long thin vein growing out of his right cheek. The other day Mr. Barnes appeared all breathless + called him off my wash stand due to a crisis in his. Pretty soon Stanley came puffing back + said "My land, I never seen Mrs. Barnes so liberal! She said she'd got to have water she didn't care if it cost a thousand dollars. So I sent Mr. Barnes into Bangor to buy a belt." About 2 hours later a very hot + tired Mr. Barnes appeared + asked Mr. Stanley to come + put on the belt. When he returned to my wash stand he said in reference to that brilliant trial lawyer Mr. Barnes "Honest some folks jist can't do a thing for themselves. Wouldn't you think every body could put on a belt!" Of course everybody knows about a Chaldean Palace.

In the middle of a hot afternoon Mr. Stanley made a laborious trip up the cellar stairs + tapped me on the shoulder + said "I may not be a millionaire but I can at least treat a girl to a plumb." And handed me a few juicy fruits. It's not often one gets a plumb from a plumber. I feel I have arrived socially with the most valuable crowd on the island.

Speaking of food. John Parker, the fire chief, popped in this morning + said "Have a piece of fried flounder". He then produced in his filthy hand two delicious fillets of sole wrapped up in a paper towel. At the Ritz they would have cost a buck fifty each. We sat down for a boney chew + a slight jaw, during which he told me about a summer visitor who was in a store in Ellsworth yesterday. While there a rather odd man, the village drunk, shuffled in, bought something, + shuffled out. The S.V. said to the store keeper "A lot of odd looking characters here aren't there?" "Yes" said the storekeeper "There are – for about 4 months and then they leave."

To-night when I hopped over to the store to git some oranges + a bottle of milk I said to Burton "You look tired". "Christ, I am" said he "what with people buying food + dying I have an awful long day. How about you comin' over + giving us a hand some night or would you be frightened to work on a body?" I gulped + allowed I'd be glad to give them a hand. He said "Good. Bodies can't do ya no harm. It's the live ones that are bothersome."

A most wonderful thing happened today. It was the aftermath of a jaunt I took yesterday p.m. Miss Manning took me over to an antique dealer friend of hers. He had a lovely cobbler's bench. I told him I ought to have it because the one that used to be here is in the Islesford Museum. We got chatting about benches + he said he'd sell me that for a hundred + twenty dollars. So we chatted on with no sale. This morning a wonderful cortege appeared. Jenny Grindle + Miss Manning bearing a wonderful cobbler's bench. "It came out of your attic" said she "+ now it has come home to roost." I am still speechless with gratitude. G.S.S.S., who happened to be passing, rushed in + sat on it + chirped "I haven't sat in this since I was a little girl + Uncle Lew sat here + I sat there + he kep his awls here + his tar here + his knives here etc etc". Apparently he had more than one bench + this was not deemed worthy of the museum. It's painted lavender + GSSS says that all the inside of the house was painted that color. It must have been something beside the red outside! When I get the rest of the house done I'm going to finish it down + have a beautiful coffee table. There is a wonderful dry sink in the shed which will be a beautiful bar. When I confided that plan to John he said "Christ, can you afford to fill all that with bottles!"

John appeared this p.m. just for a chat + helped me mix up some paint. He got talkin' + pretty soon it was 6:25. "Jesus – I gotta go or I'll be fired" said he. "Who by, your wife?" said I. "Christ no" said he "the old man. I'm clerking in the store to-day."

Before he left he told me that if he lived his father would be 87 next Christmas. "He's really too old to be working" said he. "I think he only goes to the store to wait all day so's he can count his money at night."

A Mr. Ames keeps coming to speak to John + the other day after he left I asked John about him. "Christ, he's goofy" said John. Yesterday in speaking of the Gilpin girl he said "She's goofy, but I always sorta liked her." Then he laughed + said "Guess you'll begin to think I think everybody's goofy – even you." But then he softened the blow by saying he would "carry down" an open Franklin fire to use in the "parlor". It belonged to "old Kate" + he had 2 + only used 1 + since it was a gift to him + he has a law with himself that he never sells a present this would have to be a gift + not a sale to me.

Love

R.

Day Twenty-Three/Letter 11: July 17, 1947

"GSSS . . . banged the table with her fist + said 'It makes me so cussed mad! She didn't own a tree when she came here. All she had was a suitcase'."

Rosie opened her letter of July 17, by asking and then answering the rhetorical question, "It is hard to tell which is the most fascinating day to date—but I am inclined to believe this one is. We now have a view of Sargent as well as Robinson!" She then recounts a story worthy of O. Henry about the removal of the linden tree blocking the view from *The Cobbler's* just across the road on Somes Cove.

Back on July 3, Bob Fernald had suggested to Miss Manning that she and Mrs. George Somes, proprietor of the Somes House, cut down the jointly owned Linden tree that blocked Rosie's view of Somes Cove and the mountains beyond. Directly across the street from *The Cobbler's*, the tree seemed to straddle both the Somes and the Manning properties so a joint decision was necessary. Although Miss Manning was very willing to have an axe taken to the tree, the other party, Mrs. Somes through her proxy Al Hastings, was not. Miss Manning, "after days of agitation", finally made the Solomonic decision to simply cut down her half of the tree. Al Hastings was invited to watch the procedure to "be sure it didn't take a leaf off the Somes property." Yankee respect for precisely defined property rights appears to have taken precedence over any concern for the biological welfare of the tree. The tree had two large branches sprouting from a single, jointly owned trunk. No one seemed to care whether it would survive being cut in half.

The small split-limbed linden tree in the center at the edge of Somes Cove directly opposite The Cobbler's, *some eighty-two years before becoming a local* cause celebre *(circa 1865)*

At five-thirty in the afternoon, "all hands were on deck except the woodchopper." Rosie raced over to John Fernald's house to see if he knew the whereabouts of Fred Hibbard and his axe. He did not, but on the way back Rosie met Al Hasting's brother-in-law who asked, "Are you going to chop it all down?" Rosie explained that only Miss Manning's half of the tree was being felled, to which he replied, "Why don't you chop your half down? You own it you know." Although delighted to hear that she, rather than Mrs. Somes, owned the strip of waterfront bordering the cove just across the street from her house, Rosie was, nonetheless, reluctant to "have a property fight and increase an already difficult Hastings-Parker-Somes family fight." Returning to the gathering in front of the tree, she discretely chose to remain silent about her freshly established rights to the tree. Instead, she simply welcomed Fred Hibbard, the woodchopper, who had finally arrived. But there was one more glitch. Fred had forgotten his axe, so John Fernald who had also just arrived "got the first car he saw which was Abe's funeral coach + dashed Hibbard to his place" to retrieve his axe.

They returned quickly, and Fred Hibbard began chopping. After the second swing of the axe, Mrs. Somes' proxy —Al Hastings—"proved himself of sterner metal than he knew by shouting above the ringing of the axe, "Chop it all down, Freddie". The decision delighted everyone, including Rosie's neighbor Bridgam Fernald who "dashed thru traffic + clasped Mrs. Manning by the hand + cried, 'That action is worth one thousand dollars to Somesville'." Rosie wrote "Amongst the applause I distinctly heard the Bishop's wife mutter, 'But I didn't notice him offering to pay for any of it'."

Close village living could trigger sharp tongues—usually behind a closed door or well under a speaker's breath. Rosie closes her letter by describing how upset Georgia Somes Smith Stanley was with Mrs. Somes for not being willing to cut down her half of the tree, a tree that it turned was not hers in the first place. Georgia "banged the table with her fist + said 'It makes me so cussed mad! She didn't own a tree when she came here. All she had was a suitcase. Just because she married George when he was unconscious she thinks she controls every durn tree in town'."

July 17

Dear All –

It is hard to tell which is the most fascinating day to date – but I am inclined to believe this one is. We now have a view of Sargent as well as Robinson! It came about thus. As you remember Bob had advised the two gals Mrs Somes + Miss Manning to chop down the tree. Things were at a stand still because Al Hastings couldn't be persuaded to part with it – although it was only a Linden scrub, was clogging a very hopeful young oak + and made a very blind exit to his drive. After days of agitation on Miss Manning's part it was arranged that Fred Hibbard would cut down the Manning's half. Al would watch the process to be sure it didn't take a leaf off the Somes property.

The date was set for 5:30 to-day. All hands were on deck except the woodchopper. I dashed over to John's to find out where he was. John said "Well I seen him at one o'clock to-day shingling a roof. Perhaps he fell thru the staging. If he don't show up soon I'll go look see if he did." I figured if John's idea proved true it would delay everything because John would have to take time out to bury him. However it was all a false alarm and he showed up in due course. On the way back from John's I met Al Hasting's brother-in-law who said, "Are you going to chop it all down?" I explained only Miss Manning's half. He said, "Why don't you chop your half down? You own it you know." What a bombshell! I have to check with the deed but he claims the Somes land ends with the brook + old Lew owned the strip of shore front. If true it will be nifty. However not wishing to have a property fight and increase an already difficult Hastings-Parker-Somes family fight I left the ownership of the tree out of the conversation when I returned to the site. All was ready for the first blow of the axe when it was discovered that Hibbard had forgotten his axe. John rushed + got the 1st car he saw which was Abe's funeral coach + dashed Hibbard to his place for the all vital item. Some of the crowd had dwindled when Hibbard took his first swing, but the second swing brought them all back. All Hastings proved himself of sterner metal than he knew by shouting above the ringing of the axe, "Chop it all down, Freddie." Gurgles of acclaim came from those gathered on my front steps + Mrs. Manning rushed out + waved 2 sofa pillows. On Hibbard's last stroke Bridgam Fernald dashed thru traffic + clasped Mrs Manning by the hand + cried "That action is worth 1 thousand dollars to Somesville!" Amongst the applause I distinctly heard the Bishop's wife mutter "But I don't notice him offering to pay for any of it." The fact that as the last leaf fell to earth Sargent was smothered in a thick fog has not lessened my elation at all. When complimenting Mr. Hibbard on his masterful execution I said "I could never figure out how to chop a thing like that down. And if I could figure it then I wouldn't know how to chop." "Sometimes I wish I didn't know how," said Fred gloomily + shuffled off to his supper. He was the only unenthusiastic party present.

I don't know if I wrote you during the set of discussions prior to the razing of the Linden. GSSS asked me if Mrs. Somes had been persuaded yet. When I said no she banged the table with her fist + said "It makes me so cussed mad! She didn't own a tree when she came here. All she had was a suit case. Just cause he married George when he was unconscious she thinks she controls every durn tree in town!"

Plumber Stanley + I are practically going steady now. He called out to me at noon to-day "I jist carried ya lunch into what's goin' to be your settin' room." I went in + looked + on the mantel was a large piece of birthday cake + a big bunch of grapes. After his third trip up to neighbor Barnes house to fix the belt on his pump he said "You know they're a nice family – but I guess they're just not mechanical minded."

Will write re Mr. Lawler, my newest love, tomorrow. He is the painter. He still hasn't started work partly because we can't agree on a figure + partly because he just can't get around to it.

Love

R.

Day Twenty-Six/Letter 12: July 20, 1947

"Yesterday the cupola fell into the barn . . .
the descent of the cupola is a wonderful caper."

On July 20, Rosie gave an enthusiastic progress report to her co-owners and sisters, Louisa and Frannie. Her brother, Waldo, had carefully steered clear of ownership entanglements and Frannie would eventually follow suit. Rosie had referred in an earlier letter to her co-owners as "Curator Dresser" and "Secretary to the Head of Yale". More precisely, Louisa was the curator of collections at the Worcester Art Museum and Frannie was secretary to Charlie Sawyer, the Master of Trumbull College and chairman of the Art History Department at Yale. Although a secretary, Frannie successfully prevailed on her influential and kindly boss to grant her faculty status so she could take lunch at the Faculty Club. The two sisters were confused for each other once by an indignant Yale art historian who complained to Charlie Sawyer that he had gone all the way to Chicago for a conference and who should be the featured speaker but, "That damn secretary of yours." In fact, it was Louisa, the scholar, not Frannie, the secretary, who was lecturing that day.

The list of completed projects Rosie outlined was impressive: "Mother's room + bath are finished; Hall is just about done . . . stair treads to do; ready to paint your two rooms . . . your ceilings done . . . porch is off . . . cellar is cleaned . . . boiler in." However, there was an outstanding punch list to be completed as well: "finish the painting of the 8 front rooms + . . . the kitchen . . . barn down . . . wall in back . . . cement in a few chinks in cellar against winter rats . . . have a plasterer fix 2 rooms . . . paint front of house . . . stove is a problem . . . *Window Shades* are very vital." Putting the house ahead of her hair, Rosie also asked her sisters to "cancel my perm date . . . on July 28. I don't want a perm anyway. Would rather put money into paint." She had outgrown her debutante past.

RLD's sisters and fellow owners, Frannie being rowed to Sheep Island (1993) and Louisa resting at The Cobbler's *(1950s)*

Rosie also reported that "the cupola fell into the barn", an ominous development since the barn, itself, was quite fragile and remained attached to the house. Her plan—and sisterly plea—was to have "John pull it down + salvage what lumber he can to close in the end of the ell" at the very back of the house. That was John Fernald's advice, and the "the architect son of Mrs. Barnes", the modernist Edward, agreed. So did Peter Bunker who Rosie wrote "came around (when John didn't know—they are enemies) + advised the same thing." John Fernald offered the winning point that, not only would tearing down the barn eliminate any risk to the rest of the house, "it would be cheaper to tear it down + put up a brand new barn than to salvage that one."

The full barn and cupola on the verge of collapse (1947)

So the barn was soon leveled but—to Rosie's great surprise—it happened of its own accord. Rosie learned about it when she dropped into Fernald's store and one of the storekeepers laconically asked her "How'se yah bahn doin?" Rosie said "Fine", to which he responded, "Bettah have anothah look!" She stepped outside and looking across the street was startled to discover that moments ago—and unbeknownst to her—the entire barn had finally collapsed. It has never been replaced, but every so often Rosie's nephews and neices spend a cocktail hour discussing it. So far, the spirits have yet to blind them to the practical obstacles. It may yet happen.

On Sunday, Rosie wrote home that she had taken the full day off, sleeping until eight, going to church, lunching with Nancy Greenough at the Somes House and later watching

The unobstructed view of Somes Cove and Robinson Mt. from the front parlor of The Cobbler's *after the linden tree was felled (early 1950s)*

the sailing races and going to tea at the Tysons afterwards. Charlie Tyson, president of the John A. Roebling Company, builders of the Brooklyn Bridge, was a son of the painter and collector Carroll Tyson. Over the years, he gained Rosie's unfailing respect and affection through his quiet support of virtually every important community initiative, most notably for Rosie, the Somesville Landing Corporation and the Village Improvement Association.

Towards the end of the letter, Rosie gives the impression that she is finally breaking the back of the restoration. "I wish this summer would go on for months + months + months. Our view is wonderful now we are minus the tree. I took a hot bath in the house tonight!! It is beautiful! Let's hope like Hell the water lasts!" Even the near collapse of the barn had left her unfazed. "The descent of the cupola", she wrote "is a wonderful caper."

July 20

Dear Co-owners,

To-date this is the picture:

Mother's room + bath are finished
Hall is just about done – upper + lower. Stair treads to do.
Ready to paint your two rooms right after your ceiling's done.
Held up by a bad plaster job on Living Room + Kitchen.
Parlor + room behind it yet to do – ceilings ½ done.
Porch is off – steps are on.
Cellar is cleaned with gravel on floor + boiler in.

John Lawler, the painter, came + said for 250 dollars he would paint the front + right of house + all blinds. I told him not to blow torch which will cut it down a bit. He has not started yet + I think I might get him lower if I employ him by the day instead of a project job.

Yesterday the cupola fell into the barn. The place is very unsafe. I earnestly urge that you permit me to have John pull it down + salvage what lumber he can to close in end of ell. Peter Bunker came around (when John didn't know – they are enemies) + advised same thing. John advises it. The architect son of Mrs. Barnes advises it. All the world thinks it wise. It nearly got the plumber's assistant when it fell. Barn is pulling ell with it. It breaks my heart to lose it but John says "To give you an idea what it costs it would be cheaper to tear it down + put up a brand new barn than to salvage that one." What is your pleasure? Mesdames?

I am going to finish the painting of the 8 front rooms + I hope the kitchen before I come down. I have to because it is silly to move the furniture up with no place to put it. Therefore will one of you cancel my perm date at Black + White on July 28. I don't want a perm anyway. Would rather put money into paint.

The plumber's bill has not come in. He yet has to fix the kitchen faucet.

As to the electrician – he had to connect the boiler + put in a meter to carry that load. As for his wiring, I told him we would wait on most of the plugs. I do feel it very wise to put one in Mother's room + one in the parlor + 2 upstairs where there is no light at all. Kerosene lights are ok but we have to buy these now so I figure we would be set for some time if we put in the 4. The fire hazard is reduced a bit I think.

John's bill for everything he has done to-date is in. I have paid him 75.00 because he wanted it. He probably would like the rest. I enclose same. As you will note it is 136.51 but he said he'd settle for 135.

The bathroom floor was a problem which I hope you will not think me too rash in solving by laying linoleum. That bill I also enclose.

The things which I feel are vital to do are:

Barn down
Wall in back
Cement in a few chinks in cellar against winter rats
Have a plasterer fix 2 rooms (Living room + kit)
Paint front of House

What do you think?

The shed can wait.The 2 upper ell rooms can wait. I can finish painting rest pretty soon + will come down for furniture 1st week in Aug.

The stove is a problem. We need a better elec plate than the one I'm using for more than one person. <u>Window Shades</u> are very vital since we really are right on the st + you can see in windows even in day time. Austin's in Ellsworth can supply. Shall I get a quotation on the front windows + strategic side ones?

About Furniture – you asked about a use for any double beds. I think we could bring some up – at least 2 – for future ell bedrooms. Some day there can be 2 big bedrooms there + a bath. Meantime we can store furniture there. John says front part is safe. Would you call J.C. Mader Truck Co + say we don't want truck last week in July but probably 1st in Aug.

Will write to-morrow re: fascinating call from Bridgam

also Lawler also a wonderful evening chez Stanley + several jolly chats down to AC's. It really is very entertaining + I wish this summer would go on for months + months + months. Our view is wonderful now we are minus the tree. I took a hot bath in the house tonight!! It is beautiful! Let's hope like Hell the water lasts! The descent of the cupola is a wonderful caper which I will tell you.

I took the day off to-day. Slept till 8!! Peter Bunker came around to call. Then I went to church + lunched in style on Nancy Greenough at the Somes House. Went to races + tea at Tysons. Then called on GSSS who is laid up with a bad tooth + looks like 2 children with mumps. Then Bridgam called on me. Gave me a note left by Helen Marble who came when I was out. Who is she?

Love

R.

Day Thirty-Four/Letter 13: July 28, 1947

"The house is really getting to look adorable . . ."

Rosie's next to last letter describes the painting choices. After announcing to her family that, "The house is really beginning to look adorable", she then describes room-by-room options—white, peach, yellow, foam green—all dedicated to her mother's "yen to have a light house." Yellow is the most problematic color:

> John [Fernald] doesn't like it. When I asked him why he said "It makes me homesick – I hate yellow." I can't follow his line of thought. He says his wife made him paint a lot of his house yellow + he hates yellow.

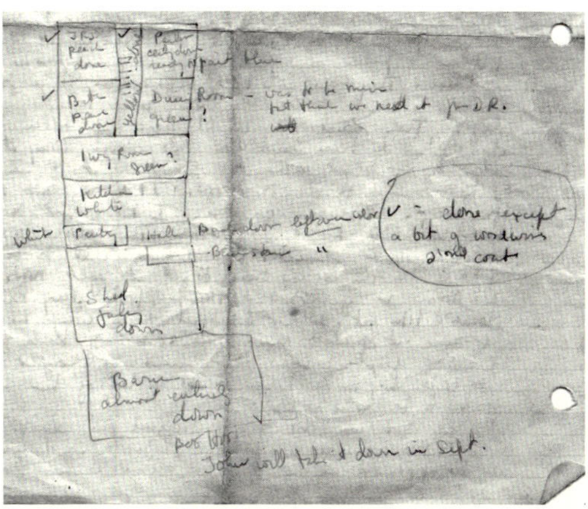

RLD's color scheme for the rooms downstairs at The Cobbler's *(1947)*

A woman of strong convictions, Rosie overrode John and "used up the living room paint on upper + lower walls – Yellow."

The painters begin: black and white on the outside; foam green, peach and yellow on the inside (1947)

Mt Desert July 28

Dear Family –

I am sorry I am not preparing to dine with Mmes Gage and Alice for a number of reasons:

1. I would like to see Alice – Give her my love + my many regrets.

2. I would like to be eating the dinner.
3. If I were there I would have had a perm.
4. Also the painting would be done.
5. And, last but not least, I would be seeing all of you.

But since I am not there I can't pretend I'm sorry to be here.

Now as to plans. The house is really getting to look adorable, but it's a slow process. I had to get a plasterer to come + fix the walls of the kitchen + patch living room + other holes in front of house. They were cute little boys whom John found – the sons of a local contractor. They were here singing, two days. They said they would pick up after them. Ha! Ha! I've been another two days doing it. I've eaten it – slept with it – breathed it + I think I have more to do tomorrow. It's no help to the painting. Ça va. I have got to redo woodwork in L's + F's rooms. The colored wood doesn't work at all. The white will be better. It's worth the extra time to get it right now. L's room is yellow + I think looks very nice. John doesn't like it. When I asked him why he said "It makes me homesick – I hate yellow". I can't quite follow his line of thought. He says his wife has made him paint a lot of his house yellow + he hates yellow.

F's room is blue + it turned out davoon!

JRD's room is peach but I'm afraid she may be disappointed in it. It seems darker than she wanted. I hope it's ok. The John (the toilet not the contractor) is peach also + now that it's a 3 piece affair is really something to behold. With hot water running in its taps it is wonderful indeed. I used up the living room paint on upper + lower halls – Yellow. (Again to John's disgust.) I think it looks very gay. I thought Mother would like it what with her yen to have a light house.

Since the porch is down we need have no worries about that! What do you all say to a foam green living room. If you don't approve let me know. I'm working on the stairs now + they're some job! I shall tackle kitchen next. Here is chart of condition of things. [*she refers to the color scheme shown on p.138.*]

Moving day (1947)

Day Thirty-Seven/Letter 14: August 1, 1947

"Today has been a perfect day. It's really the first all summer. You can see every tree on Sargeant. It's cold, but all the same I went in swimming. It was davoon."

In Rosie's final letter and as the restoration nears an end, she beams, "Today has been a perfect day. It's really the first all summer. You can see every tree on Sargent. It's cold, but all the same I went in swimming. It was davoon."

Dr. and Mrs. Walter Seelye paid a visit from Little Cranberry and brought a guest log as a housewarming present. The wood-bound book remains in use today at *The Cobbler's*, although it has been supplemented over the years. Rosie considered the Seelyes "my best public because every time they come they go over the whole house + notice what's been done." Paying them the highest compliment, she wrote "They are as good as a cocktail when they come."

This engaging final letter includes a comic episode that might have been a Monty Python sketch. Bishop Manning asked Rosie to join a small and eclectic group for a morning viewing in Bar Harbor of *Black Narcissus*, the controversial Michael Powell/Eric Pressburger film that had deeply offended the Catholic Church in the United States. Rank, the English producers, got it in their fuzzy heads that the Episcopalians, whose leader in New York was Bishop

Manning, might take a more enlightened view than the Catholic hierarchy. Evidently, the Rank Public Relations Department had not done much homework on Bishop Manning when they asked him to bless their film. Seven years earlier he had led the fight against Bertrand Russell's appointment to the Philosophy Department at the College of the City of New York by denouncing the liberal, distinguished and, some would say, libertine English philosopher as "lecherous, venomous, erotomaniac, aphrodisiac, atheistic, irreverent, narrow-minded, untruthful and bereft of moral fibre." *Black Narcissus* never had a prayer.

Bishop Manning in his prime as leader of the Episcopal Church in New York (Pach Brothers, 1940s)

The entourage included "Margaret Barnes to come + judge it for literary value, a Mr. Stimson because he's a head vestryman . . . an Anglican priest named Father Lang + . . . me." Mr. Stimson was Freddy Stimson, a Somesville resident and nephew of Henry, the former Secretary of War who had recently published an article in *Harper's* that was the first public defense of the Administration's decision to drop nuclear bombs on civilians in Hiroshima and Nagasaki. Although never mentioned in the letters, the war was always close at hand.

As Rosie reported, Powell's film failed, not only with "the Bish" on spiritual grounds but with her as entertainment.

> When it was over we waited breathlessly for the Bish's opinion. He rose to his feet (which is not a very impressive gesture with him because his legs are so short that the net result is still only 5 ft 2. He really needs a pulpit.) He let the axe fall + intoned, "I cannot endorse the picture. It seems to show the defeat of the Church by the world."

Rosie concluded less apocalyptically that, "Personally, I thought it was such a slow dull movie that I couldn't greatly care whether the world of the flesh or the spirit triumphed. It would have been better to have stayed home with my paint brush. But the whole deal was amusing. In spite of my day I managed to paint the kitchen ceiling." There was no such silver lining for the Rank Public Relations executive who had flown to Mt. Desert for the Bishop's support. He left empty-handed the next day.

On the July 30 there had been "a gala evening . . . to raise money for the Village Improvement Society . . . including a magnificent production of *Iolanthe* given by the school children." Rosie had "spent .65 on a ticket but refrained from bidding $9 for a chocolate cake because I felt we were improving the village sufficiently by painting *The Cobbler's*."

Somesville's Village Improvement Society was a mainstay of community life, an opportunity for residents—local and summer—to raise funds for the general "improvement" of the village. The island of Mt. Desert was divided then, as it is now, into four townships, each a fully constituted political entity with its own elected officials. They are the towns of Bar Harbor, Mt. Desert, Southwest Harbor and Tremont. Mt. Desert, the township, includes the villages of Northeast Harbor, Seal Harbor, Pretty Marsh and Somesville. The villages themselves have no formal status, and cannot tax residents for additional local services not otherwise provided by the township.

As a result, civic organizations like the Village Improvement Society—and the Somesville Landing Corporation and the Volunteer Fire Department—play a vital community role by raising money to support services not provided by the town. Fortunately, "white elephant sales", "blueberry pancake breakfasts", performances of *Iolanthe*, cake sales, games of beano and voluntary donations—the lifeblood of these organizations—have proved to be effective and appealing alternatives to mandatory increases in property taxes. In 1948, the year following this particular "gala evening", Rosie began her long involvement with the Village Improvement Association by assuming responsibility for the annual theatrical production. Many years later she became the anomalous summer resident presiding over the Village Improvement Society. As her friend Anne Biddle Mikhalapov jokingly said, "That made Rosie the Mayor of

Ga performing, RLD directing, If Women Worked As Men Do *at the Village Improvement Association's annual carnival (1948)*

Somesville."

The letter also refers to a "list of furniture . . . with hints and hopes" that Rosie had sent home earlier as she began thinking about furnishing *The Cobbler's.* Most of her "hints + hopes" were easily satisfied because 49 Elm Street at the time was a virtual museum, overflowing with generations of family artifacts. *The Cobbler's* would soon be filled with fine nineteenth century furniture, suitable to a house built in 1852. This letter outlines the first of what would be over forty years of annual furniture shuffles between Massachusetts, Connecticut and Maine.

Rosie came from a family of savers. Generation after generation, little was thrown away—especially furniture, china, portraits and letters. As one generation died, the younger generation simply moved their second string pieces into backrooms or into second houses. Rosie, with her sister Louisa's acquiesence, took this migratory game to an extreme. By the 1970s, Rosie and Louisa maintained six residences, owning five of them, three together. They had two houses in Worcester, a farmhouse on the common in Woodstock, an apartment on Buckingham Street in Cambridge, a small camp on their small island in Somes Harbor and *The Cobbler's.* Oscar Wilde's Lady Bracknell would certainly have approved. "Three addresses always inspire confidence," she told a prospective niece.

Rosie would spend hours each spring diagramming multi-state moves in what amounted to a three-dimensional game of furniture chess. Moving one piece usually triggered an exponential series of counter moves in multiple directions and on different levels. Three states and six houses complicated things. The acquisition in 1965 of Sheep Island in Somesville added a whole new dimension to an already complex yearly undertaking: the need to transport furniture across Somes Harbor. A typical move might involve transporting, say, a Hepplewhite bureau from Woodstock to Worcester in exchange for a Federal sofa that would then be transported to *The Cobbler's* in Somesville replacing a tired settee that would be rowed across the harbor to the camp on Sheep Island where it would seem magically rejuvenated —everything being relative. Hours of planning and weeks of scheduling would go into these moves, each of which was as predictable as the Caribou roaming north across the Yukon each spring.

Rosie ended her final letter by describing "an elderly Russian Refugee who lives next door" and "stops in twice a day to give me a few comments. She speaks atrocious

French + no English." Rosie noted, "she was getting on my nerves terribly when all of a sudden she asked me to dine with her at the Somes House." A hungry opportunist, Rosie "took my atrocious French right over there with my tongue hanging out over dinner." They "met a friend of Mother's, Mrs. MacInnes, who sent her love and wants to see her." That short visit epitomized Rosie's Somesville, a perpetually refreshing mix of familiar ground and fresh, new territory.

Ga picnicking with the "good as a cocktail" Seelyes on Little Cranberry (early 1950s)

August 1

Dear All –

I feel I have let you all down terribly by not getting down to pack up van. Is it OK? I enclose the list of furniture we made out once before with a few additions, deletions and hints + hopes. Change it as you all think wisest.

I'm sorry to have let you down so much in the achievement of the paint job. It all takes a long time. And after my labors it doesn't look so good either. But I improve. I hope I have not made too many wrong decisions. If I have, another coat of paint will probably undo the damage. The month has been a strain muscularly, but not mentally. I only wish it was June 15 again instead of August 1.

Today has been a perfect day. It's really the first all summer. You can see every tree on Sargeant. It's cold, but all the same I went in swimming. It was davoon.

Dr. and Mrs. Seelye called again today + brought us all a present – a guest log. They are my best public because every time they come they go over the whole house + notice what's been done. Also they are the only two people who appreciate that there is more labor in sanding woodwork + pulling carpet tacks than there is in spreading on a bright blue paint. So they are as good as a cocktail when they come.

Speaking of cocktails I went to a very fancy party yesterday. Miss Manning entertained for her sister, Mrs. Geoffrey Cole. I put on a dress for the occasion + everybody tippled in style. That evening I went on a picnic to Seawall supposedly to see the moon rise but instead we were all treated to a thunderstorm. To add to a day of no work I went in the morning to a special showing of "Black Narcissus". Apparently the Catholic Church has condemned the movie so the Rank Producers (who gave the world Henry V, Brief Encounter + a few others) flew up the film + rented a theatre in Bar Harbor to have Bishop Manning give it the Protestant blessing. When he asked the theatre manager how many he could invite he said 900. He contented himself with 9. He asked Margaret Barnes to come + judge it for literary value, a Mr. Stimson because he's a head vestry man or something somewhere + an Anglican priest named Father Lang + since there was an extra seat in the car they took me. We had our pick of seats. The Rank public relations man explained the Hollywood dilemma, we went in + took our choice of seats + the show started. When it was over we waited breathlessly for the Bish's opinion. He rose to his feet (which is not a very impressive gesture with him because his legs are so short that the net result is still only 5 ft 2. He really needs a pulpit.) He let the axe fall + intoned, "I cannot endorse the picture. It seems to show the defeat of the Church by the world." Then he sailed forth to his auto + the poor public relations man gathered himself + his film together + flew back to N.Y. Personally, I thought it was such a slow dull movie that I couldn't greatly care whether the world of the flesh or the spirit triumphed. It would have been better to have stayed home with my paint brush. But the whole deal was amusing. In spite of my day I managed to paint the kitchen ceiling.

Night before last was a gala evening because there was a carnival in the town hall to raise money for the Village Improvement Society. There was a magnificent production of *Iolanthe* given by the school children. It was followed by Beano, auction, games etc etc etc up until 11:30! I spent .65 on a ticket but refrained from bidding $9 for a chocolate cake because I felt we were improving the village sufficiently by painting "The Cobbler's".

The other day when I went to the store to buy my ration of milk, bread + lettuce Bob waited on me. He picked up a sales slip pad + wrote my names on it saying "Rosa Dresser – Grade A." My spirits soared to the sky. I thought "great compliment". He repeated it, "Rosa Dresser, Grade A" I soared some more. Then I heard him say "Grade A Macaroni". I am deflated. He came in to see how I was making out yesterday. I displayed the front hall with pride. I had just finished the 2nd coat on the woodwork + it was glowing + beautiful, I thought. His comment was – "Hey, Rosa, you're goin' to put a second coat on this, aren't ya?" That on top of the macaroni was too much.

To-day Mr. Lawler + his boys started to paint the outside of the store. I said, "Oh, Mr. Lawler are you leaving already? When will I see you next?" He stopped his truck with a screech of breaks + called out, "About November." With that Bob burst out of the store + said "G'wan Johnny, why don't you say this evenin'?" "Wouldn't dare", shouted Johnny, "Might find you callin' on her." And he + his boys fled to So-west Habah leaving me to gather up my dignity in the middle of Main St. I think GSSS has spread it about that Johnny Lawler + I would be a good match. He's a bachelor + I'm an old maid. Benton told me that there had only been 4 weddings in the Somesville church + it would be nice to have a 5th. I don't know but what matrimony with Lawler would be a solution to the paint bill. And it would make the Fernalds so happy.

GSSS came in to-day to chew a little fat. Her abscess is better + she can get in her dentures again so she likes a little gossip every once in a way (i.e. about every time she passes the house.) To-day she got laughing over Ethel Fernald Badger. I remarked that she had never spoken to me. "Although", I said, "Her father's been over to call several times." She rolled her eyes with a little leer + said, "Did he hug you yet? You want to watch out for him. He's been huggin' all his life. He's in his 90th year + and he's still a huggin' when he gets a chance." He came to admire my paint job the other day + said "Do you take that from your mother or your father?" It somehow seems to lend such dignity to paint slapping as if it were a beautiful voice or blond curly hair. Did I tell you that one day he said, "I'm 89 years old + stone deaf – but there's nothing wrong with my eyes." I took the hint + hung a sheet over the bathroom window. Somes

Smith dropped in for a call the other evenin + stayed 3 hours. That was a little too much of a good thing. But he told me a lot of gossip + read me a few poems he had written. Do you remember his gem that Harry Somes showed us? "a land that my fore-fathers founded + christened it Mt Desert Maine"?

There is an elderly Russian Refugee who lives next door chez M. Parker. She stops in twice a day to give me a few comments. She speaks atrocious French + no English. She was getting on my nerves terribly when all of a sudden she asked me to dine with her at the Somes House. I took my atrocious French right over there with my tongue hanging out over it at dinner. I met a friend of Mother's, Mrs. MacInnes, who sent her love and wants to see her.

Love R.

The Cobbler's *restored (early 1950s)*

The Final Months of 1947

Rosie's mother and sister Frannie arrived in Somesville on August 13 bringing a natural end to this particular cycle of letters. They were delighted by the Herculean success Rosie had achieved during the first two months of the summer. The house was more than livable. As Rosie had promised, it was "adorable". On Saturday, September 16, a moving truck arrived from Worcester with sixty-seven items, all extracted from cavernous 49 Elm Street. Winsor chairs, a high boy, a girandole, mirrors, a rush bottom rocker, a black walnut rocker, a medicine cabinet, andirons, an oil painting by Ernest Wadsworth Longfellow, a feather bed and a wing chair were all part of the loot transferred from the attic, guest rooms and library at 49 Elm to *The Cobbler's.*

Much has been added to the house since then, but remarkably little of the original haul from 49 Elm has been removed. As elderly aunts and uncles died, Rosie continued to feed *The Cobbler's* with ancestral artifacts. But the overall effect remained unchanged: New England Federalist. Austere, softened by nineteenth century travel souvenirs such as a tile stolen a century earlier from the Alhambra and walls of prints, paintings and photographs. In describing *The Cobbler's*, a 1995 guide noted, "The interior of this house is remarkably preserved. Its front parlor is a beautifully proportioned, modest Federal room." Although, the interior might better be described as restored than preserved, the guide captures the feeling of the house both today and back in the early fall of 1947 when Rosie completed the first phase of her restoration.

In describing the restored house, a realtor might boldly spin it as "a center staircase 'Greek Revival Cape-style house' with seven bedrooms, two full baths, a parlor, a living room, a kitchen and a dining room". But that would give the wrong impression. *The Cobbler's* is a small house with tiny rooms and relatively low ceilings. That helped keep the house warm in the winter, but it could make for close living. Geoffrey Biddle, the young son of a close friend of Rosie's, entered one of the downstairs bedrooms and announced to his mother and Rosie, "They have wall-to-wall bedding!" Quarters were tight, a sharp contrast to the elegant Greek Revival mansion house that Rosie had grown up in as a child. But after the trauma of war, architectural intimacy must have been just what she was looking for in a house.

On October 17—with her family back home in Worcester and Rosie still in Somesville—a fire broke out just north of Bar Harbor, some eight miles east of Somesville. It burned for twenty-eight days, destroying 237 homes and burning some 17,188 acres. Although much of Bar Harbor was devastated, Somesville was spared. The French newspaper *Le Figaro* reported wishfully that local "peasants" had set the fire to destroy the great estates of the rich. In fact, the Depression, World War II and the Internal Revenue Service had already brought an end to the Newport grandiosity of Bar Harbor. The famous fire only punctuated the inevitable. Mt. Desert was becoming a playground for the many as well as "We Happy Few". Rosie was more than ready to make the transition.

"The woods were already filled with shadows one June evening, just before eight o'clock, although a bright sunset still glimmered fairly among the trunks of the tree."

Sarah Orne Jewett, *A White Heron*

chapter FIVE

Epilogue

RLD relaxing—at last—in the back shed room of The Cobbler's *(early 1960s)*

Rosie spent each of her next forty-two summers in Somesville. In 1948, she joined the Winsor School faculty in Boston as director of the Drama Department, eventually becoming head of the Fine Arts Department and, from 1963 until her retirement in 1973, the head of the Upper School. Throughout the 1950s her life triangulated between Boston, Worcester and Mt. Desert. In 1964 she added Woodstock, Connecticut to the mix. Rosie was so involved in each of the four communities—both socially and organizationally—that it seemed as if she were a full-time resident of each.

She sublet an apartment in Cambridge at 2 Buckingham Street from her friend Pamela Taylor, the wife of Francis Henry Taylor who had been director of the Metropolitan Museum and twice served as director of the Worcester Art Museum. During the school year, Pamela lived in Florence where she was head of the Villa Mercedi. She returned to Cambridge each summer, whereupon Rosie would depart for Maine. The apartment was filled with European drawings, dark bronze sculptures and finely bound books belonging to the Taylors. The living room looked out on a small garden filled with rhododendron, protected by an elegant fence and maintained by another family, the Constables.

Buckingham Street was a refreshing foil to the ancestral

density of Worcester. In 1950, 49 Elm Street—the so-called Lincoln Mansion—was sold to the Worcester Mutual Fire Insurance Company of which Levi Lincoln II had been the first president. They wanted the valuable downtown land, not the old house, and agreed to let Old Sturbridge Village and Treadway Inns move the front of the building to Sturbridge where it stands today—its Greek columns still intact but missing both wings and virtually all its original detail. Rosie's mother, Ga, and Louisa, moved into a much smaller house at 65 Wachusett Street that was a short walk from the Worcester Art Museum where Louisa managed the collections by day and produced original scholarship late into the night.

In a feat of organizational magic, most of the contents of 49 Elm were squeezed into 65 Wachusett, although major pieces of furniture were farmed out on loan to relatives. Rosie kept a room there and used it regularly when she came to Worcester for cocktail parties, meetings of the Shakespeare Club and Sunday lunch. Rosie, the very early bird, and Louisa, the scholarly night owl, kept radically different schedules. Late one night—or early one morning—the house erupted in loud voices when Rosie and Weezie met at the front door, and began arguing whether a cocktail party at the Stoddards was "tonight" or "tomorrow night". Rosie was on her way out the door to drive to Winsor and thought it was "tonight". Louisa was just returning from a night of research at the museum and thought the party was "tomorrow". In a relative sense, they were both right.

The close quarters at 65 Wachusett tightened even

more in 1962 when Rosie's sister Frannie, her husband John and their three children moved in while their new glass house—designed by John—was being built off of Salisbury Street. Not surprisingly, construction that was expected to take nine months, took almost eighteen. The three sisters —Rosie, Louisa and Frannie—were together again, setting off occasional sparks that were gracefully doused by their mother and which were celebrated by Rosie in a Christmas Eve production entitled *The Three Scrooges.* It captures the spirited complexity of New England tribal living and shows off Rosie's playful but pointed humor.

The Three Scrooges: Frannie Herron, Louisa Dresser, and RLD (early 1982)

The Three Scrooges by Rose L. Dresser

'Twas two days before Christmas and all through the house,
Not a creature was stirring – not even the Louse.
The place was a mess, an unspeakable sight,
But the hope was Elzena would soon put it right.
Some Dressers and Herrons were tucked into bed.
The extras were curled on the carpet instead.
Ga in her four poster, the cat in her lap,
Had just settled down for a little cat nap.
When came the dawn – the alarm rang a clatter,
And up rose Rosie as Mad as a Hatter.
"The milk man's not come and there's nothing for food!
What on earth shall we feed the young Herron brood?"
Frannie yelled from her bed: "There's no time for eating!
They've got to be scrubbed for All Saints Sunday Meeting!
Unitarians, true, may not get to Heaven,
But at least they don't pray till almost eleven.
This service at nine, ears washed and shoes polished,
Is something Pope Hastings should have abolished."
"There are too many cooks in this kitchen", snarled Rose,
"The sauce pans are stored with the boys winter clothes!"
Crash!!! Crash!!!
Then Louisa rushed by with some letters to mail,'
And Josephine set up a shattering wail;
"I can't find my petticoat – Jock has my mitten!
And Frank drank the milk that was meant for the kitten!"
When what to all wondering eyes should appear,
But the *Pater Familias*, full of good cheer.
As rapid as turtles, the children they came.
He whistled and shouted and called them by name,
"Come on Jock! Come on Jo! And Frank, get your Bible.
Good-bye Ga, good-bye girls. This life is so TRIBAL."
And into the Falcon all piled at his call,
They dashed away, dashed away, dashed away all.
The Three Scrooges sat down and thought they'd relax,

But soon they were at it, hammer and tacks.
"I think for Christmas," Louisa began,
"We all ought to act as sweet as we can.
Rosie, you wrap the presents, and Frannie, you cook.
I have to give the Museum a look."
"But wait up," cried Frannie, "We haven't begun,
To plan for our party and gay Christmas fun."
"What we need is a tree," Rosie said with a Grrrrr,
"But there's nothing but spruces and John wants a fir."
Louisa spoke up – she was happy and calm,
"I've ordered a tree from George, Richard and Tom."
"Yes," Rosie snarled, "but you bought one so small,
It's more like a corsage for the Thanksgiving ball!"
"We've got to get started without more delay!
Are we going to sit here drinking coffee all day?
What are you doing? That's my coffee cup!
I'm not nearly finished. Don't start to pick up!"
"Don't empty the dishwasher, you old...baboon.
Things haven't been washed yet. Give me that spoon!"
"Of course they've been washed. I ran it myself.
I'm putting these dishes right back on the shelf."
"Stop fighting, I tell you, we've got to make plans.
There's that party to go to and the kids on our hands."
"So, I don't know if Mother is going or not.
She must have a fever, She seems kind of hot.
The thermometer's broken, so how will we know,
Whether or not she should stay here or go?"
"I'll do what you want to make the plans fit.
Do I go to the party or do I babysit?"
"Tuesday is Christmas! My shopping's not done!
And as for my cards, I haven't sent one!"
"I'm giving a party tomorrow at six.
There's food to be ordered and hors d'oeuvres to fix."
Just then Ga appeared and she had her say:
"Why don't we simply skip the whole Day?"

The Three Roses: Josephine Rose Lincoln Dresser with her daughter Rose Lincoln Dresser in 1909 and her feisty granddaughter Josephine Rose Lincoln Herron in 1954

The annual Christmas Eve party and pageant was one of numerous celebrations that the Dressers carried over with little modification from cavernous 49 Elm to cramped 65 Wachusett. The inclusive guest list, the costumes, the format, the exuberance were the same. One Christmas, the tree at 65 Wachusett—cut at the Waldo Dresser tree farm in Jefferson—was lit with real candles using antique glass ornaments that once lit the Christmas trees at 49 Elm. When it came to parties, the Dressers crept into the twentieth century. Although they liked their own liquor unadulterated—usually, neat Scotch or gin lightly scented with vermouth—they also served ancient New England punches in large porcelain bowls that sat on mahogany sideboards like Shinto offerings

The Sunday Lunch Crowd: the "three good boys"—Tom, George and Richard Dresser standing behind their city-slicker cousins—Jock, Frank, and Josephine Herron (mid 1950s)

to ancestral gods. Experienced guests avoided them.

The beacon for the extended family was Rosie's mother, Ga. An elegant woman with sparkling eyes and a playful wit, Ga had that rare capacity to make anyone in a room —whether three, thirty or ninety years old—feel like the star attraction. The phrase *grande dame* is now quaint, but Ga embodied it with grace, understatement and mischievous good humor. Most every Sunday, she hosted a formal Sunday lunch for her children, grandchildren and stray cousins, family friends and visitors. The Herron boys were dressed in starched white shirts, sharply pressed gray flannels, and patent leather shoes that sparkled in the sun. Their sister, Josephine, usually wore a floral bonnet and a deep blue velvet dress fluffed by petticoats. Their Dresser cousins, on the other hand, had the benefit of growing up in the country where the dress code was more generous. The envy of the Herron children, the Dresser boys wore clean plaid shirts, sturdy pants and handsome boots to the formal Sunday lunches. While the adults drank cocktails in a room filled with portraits, the grandchildren scrambled about the house, spilling ginger ale, exploring a large attic and playing a game of bowling on a miniature set made in an earlier century. At lunch, the generations were rejoined at a large, ever expanding table that was set with old china, silver and crystal. Even the servant bells were brilliantly polished. But they were set out for fun. The only people slaving in the kitchen were aunts and obliging guests. The help was long gone.

During these Sunday lunches, family stories were told over and over and over again: visually impaired Levi Lincoln I tossing dimes from his carriage at geese that he mistook for poor children; Josephine Rose travelling as an infant from malarial Antigua to Salem in a shoebox; Emma Dresser overhearing a Woodstock in-law criticizing the Holt family as inbred and imperious as she relaxed on the deck of an ocean liner bound for Venice; Daniel Waldo, Worcester's first banker, walking ten miles to Leicester to retrieve ten cents due from a borrower; young Paine cousins ruining a Winthrop Chandler portrait of Judge Timothy Paine by using it as a dartboard in the nineteenth century; Daniel Waldo Lincoln being thrown from his observation car and killed while watching the Harvard-Yale rowing races in New London; George Bancroft hugging one of Waldo Lincoln's children and exclaiming, "Now, he can say he's been held by a great man"; Frank Dresser referring to his spry great-grandfather as "Boom Boom" and his infirm grandfather as "Sick Boom Boom"; Levi Lincoln II's wife, Penelope Winslow Sever, feeding a full military company at 49 Elm Street when the Commander misinterpreted a personal invitation that read, "the pleasure of your company is requested for dinner." On, and irrepressibly on, they went.

Ga in her Hunting Rose tartan on Somes Sound (late 1950s)

These festive Sunday lunches—enlivened by games of "Button, Button" and "Hunt the Thimble"—came to an end in 1965 as Ga's health began to deteriorate. On November 20, a headline on the front page of the *Worcester Telegram* announced what was simultaneously unthinkable and inevitable, "Death Takes Mrs. Dresser at 87". Another headline late that afternoon in the *Worcester Evening Gazette* reported,

"Prominent Foundress of Drama Group Dies". After a long and richly engaged life, Ga had finally succumbed to cancer. Her husband, Frank Farnum Dresser, had died 41 years earlier, and she had never remarried. Instead, she spent the rest of her life shepherding a growing family through the Depression, a world war and the evolving American landscape of the 1950s.

She handled the transition from nineteenth century privilege to twentieth century domesticity with grace. Recalling their mother's management of 49 Elm after most of the help was gone, Rosie's sister, Frannie Herron, wrote in her recollection, "The Lincoln House", that "Mother used to sweep around the kitchen bundled up in a tattered mink cape, about the same vintage as the house, and we thought she looked terribly grand as she stirred the soup." Writing in the *Worcester Magazine* some years later, local historian Albert Southwick recalled "Josephine Rose Lincoln Dresser . . . at the elegant old Lincoln Mansion . . . in the great oak-paneled living room . . . redolent with history . . . the Dresser women, mothers and daughters, seem[ed] to be from an earlier, more gracious time." Over cocktails some years later, the three sisters concluded that Ga had the best attributes of each —the braininess and good judgment of Louisa, the theatrical energy of Rosie and the social grace of Frannie. She also had the dry and very wry humor of her son, Waldo.

The mid-1960s proved to be a robust period for Rosie. Having survived a year and a half with the Herron family at 65 Wachusett Street and, sadly, the death of her mother, she began to expand her property holdings. In 1964, Rosie

Belmawr, *RLD's country retreat in Woodstock, CT (early 1990s)*

and Louisa inherited an 1820 farmhouse on the common of Woodstock Hill in northeastern Connecticut from their uncle George Chandler Lincoln as well as a good inheritance that finally gave Rosie some financial breathing room. Although Uncle George had expected his nieces to sell the house once its contents were distributed, Rosie convinced Louisa to keep it. Rosie would use it as a country house on weekends away from Cambridge during the school year, and Louisa would get the opportunity to store her things and subsidize the upkeep throughout the year.

More adventurously, Rosie then convinced her sister Louisa to take part of their inheritance and use it to purchase Sheep Island, an eight-acre island with a small cabin and a dock in the middle of Somes Harbor. Rosie had covetously eyed Sheep Island—as well as the Somes House—for many years. Every summer she rowed over to visit the owner, Virginia Somes Sanderson, to inquire about it.

The view down the Sound from the camp on Sheep Island (1980s)

Serendipitously, Miss Sanderson—a professor at Ohio State University and a generous benefactor of her hometown of Somesville—decided to sell just as Uncle George's bequests cleared probate. She gave Rosie a weekend's head start to make the purchase before the island was put on the open market. Rosie moved quickly. Partnering with her friend, Fred Fraley, she bought the island and a small point of land also owned by Miss Sanderson that was directly across from Sheep. The Fraleys acquired the small point of land since it abutted their own property on the eastern shore of Somes Harbor, and Rosie—after years on the hunt—took possession of the island itself with her sister. Rosie's great aunt—the Worcester real estate maven—Frances Merrick Lincoln, would have been delighted.

The nearly simultaneous addition of Woodstock and Sheep Island added rich logistical complexity to Rosie's life.

Epilogue

Until she retired from the Winsor School in 1973 and made Woodstock rather than Cambridge (and, briefly, Weston) her home base, the Woodstock house was used primarily for family holidays such as Thanksgiving and Easter, birthday parties and occasional country weekends. Managing these periodic celebrations from afar was challenging, even for someone as well organized as Rosie. One year she set the Thanksgiving tables in September only to discover when she arrived in Woodstock the night before Thanksgiving that she had to wash the dust off everything—plates, silver and glass—for forty guests. Equal parts shrine and warehouse, the house was used for the first decade to store some of the finest pieces from 49 Elm—Federal furniture, ten of the best portraits, enough china for a state dinner and semi-organized piles of eclectic family debris including the fourteen letters which inspired this book. The piles were really more like small mesas since they formed the better part of what is now a seventy-thousand piece collection of family papers. Rosie's storage was so efficient, that it took her exhausted heirs eight family divisions to divide her property in Woodstock—or most of it. In 2004, over a decade after Rosie's death, a dozen steamer trunks still remain undivided—and unopened—in the large barn behind the house.

Sheep Island became a major project for Rosie. Although the cabin had no electricity, it did have a propane operated icebox, hot water heater and stove. The cabin was lit at night by kerosene lamps and heated, on rare occasions, by a large fireplace in the living room. The water system included a well-house and pump in the center of the island that fed an ungainly water tower that looked as if it should have been on a west Texas ranch. The island had a warren of trails running through it and a small graveyard where two infants had been buried in 1874. The dock and the house were on the southernmost tip of the island, leaving the rest of it "wild" except for the trails and several intimidating "No Trespassing" signs posted by Rosie. The highpoint of the house was a well-sheltered screen porch looking out on the harbor and "the Westerns"—Mansell and Bernard mountains, in National Park-speak. Every chance she had, Rosie would use the porch for evening cocktails, surveying the harbor and luxuriating in the setting sun. As *Bar Harbor Times* reporter, Nan Lincoln, later wrote, Rosie "frequently used [Sheep Island] as a great escape, by rowboat, from such intrusive amenities as telephones and electricity." It was Rosie's refuge from a busy life.

The interior of the cabin was simple—a primitive kitchen, two bedrooms, a bathroom, several closets and a large living room with a massive fireplace that was used with great care for fear that sparks floating up the chimney might land on flammable trees outside. Two decorative themes dominated the cabin: nautical charts and sheep. The latter included everything from old advertisements featuring sheep to an oil painting by Albrecht Schenck of a fierce ram in a thick snowstorm. A large nineteenth century engraving after Courbet hung over the fireplace. In it, a flock of apprehensive sheep are being rowed to an uncertain destination—perhaps for shearing, perhaps for slaughter, perhaps simply to graze over fresh fields. Destiny was in the

The two faces of Sheep Island: quiet glades and lively dinners

eye of the beholder. A plumber had saved the print from a damp barn vacated by a distant Peabody cousin of Rosie's in Northeast Harbor. Improbably, it was identical to one that Rosie's mother had received as a wedding gift, presumably from the same source, presumably at the same time and presumably for the same purpose at the turn of the century.

Life was not always idyllic on Sheep Island. One morning around six-thirty, just as the sun was beginning to ease through the fog, Rosie woke a young nephew who was sleeping on the porch and cursed, "Country living is for the birds!" She had been out at the water tower trying to put in a new water filter, but could not get the old one out. A beautiful day was dawning, but she was too cross to notice. Nonetheless, Sheep Island was special. A short row across Somes Harbor, it was her private haven, her temporary shelter from social commitments on the larger island and, more importantly, the growing summer traffic that was making

The Cobbler's less peaceful, except in the shed room at the very back of the house or during the off-season.

Rosie took great pride in Sheep Island, and was viscerally annoyed whenever it was left off a detailed map. At the Jordan Pond Teahouse in Seal Harbor, a thirty square-foot topographical map of Mt. Desert graced the restaurant entrance so tourists could site themselves geographically while waiting in long lines to be seated for tea and popovers. Noticing that Sheep Island was missing from the map, Rosie marched into the gift shop, bought a pack of chewing gum, chewed several sticks of it and planted the masticated goo on the map right in Somes Harbor where Sheep Island belonged. Fortunately, no Winsor students were standing nearby to see the normally correct head of their Upper School take local cartography into her own hands—and mouth.

A typical year in Somesville for Rosie would begin—or end—in the dark of winter at a New Year's house party given by Reggie Allen and Helen Howe Allen. Reggie was a leading Gilbert & Sullivan scholar and the first general manager of Lincoln Center. Helen was a popular monologist as well as an accomplished novelist who wrote *The Gentle Americans*, nominally a biography of her father Mark deWolfe Howe, but essentially a eulogy to nineteenth century Brahmin Boston, a world Rosie knew well. Two other couples usually joined them: Bob and Barbara Patterson and Robert and Judith Mitchell. Bob was a leading architect on Mt. Desert who had joined with Rosie, Reggie and others to create the Somesville Landing Corporation. The civic legacy Bob left his adopted state is diverse and enduring. He helped establish the Allagash Wilderness Waterway and led the campaign to rebuild the Jordan Pond Tea House after it burned down. He also preserved much of Beatrix Farrand's lifework by transplanting prime cuttings from her famous Reef Point garden in Bar Harbor to the Thuya and the Azalea Gardens in Northeast Harbor. His wife, Barbara, was an expert birder dedicated to preserving wildlife habitats on the fast growing island of Mt. Desert and in the vulnerable north woods along the Allagash. The Mitchells had moved from New York in the 1930s to Placentia Island, purchasing the three hundred acre island just off of Bass Harbor to live the "back-to-nature" life that Helen and Scott Nearing popularized three decades later. For many years, the only night the Mitchells spent off Placentia was celebrating New Year's in Somesville with the Allens, the Pattersons and Rosie.

Following New Year's, Rosie's next trip Down East would be a weekend in late spring to get the house ready. Then—in June, while she was still teaching, or in May, when she had retired—Rosie would move north for the summer. When she was teaching at Winsor, she would leave for Somesville almost literally from the school parking lot as commencement ceremonies ended. Her summer calendar—always a Phillips Brooks calendar—tracked a dense schedule of cocktail parties, visits from workmen, house parties, organizational meetings, the arrival and departure of family and friends. Until her death in 1965, Rosie's mother spent the entire summer at *The Cobbler's,* and each year Rosie's brother, Waldo, and her sister, Frannie, visited with their rambunctious families. Rosie gave numerous house parties including a spirited annual weekend in which she and each of her guests—Kit and Bill Wheeler, John Curtis, Bob Booth, Russell Stobbs and her cousin Channie Johnson—followed the quaint protocol of calling each other by their middle names—Augustus, Whitin, Weld, Murdoch, Chandler, Lincoln—for the entire weekend. When Rosie was in residence, Somesville was also a popular destination for many of her sailing friends—George Bullock, Ollie Chute, Dick and Ann Prouty, Buzz and Sallie Knowlton, Henry Slack and Tuna Holt—who would change crews, wash their clothes and share a lively meal out on Sheep Island or at *The Cobbler's* as they celebrated the end of a long cruise. When the house was full, Rosie would have Agnes Grant prepare

The Dresser and Herron families outside The Cobbler's *with Ga center stage (early 1960s)*

breakfasts for everyone beginning around seven. Rosie got the vacation ball rolling early.

Each summer day was dense with action. Mountains were usually climbed in the morning, often before breakfast. There might be a late morning row over to Sheep or a quick marketing trip to Northeast or Southwest, usually for a non-essential item. Lunch might be a picnic at Seawall, a sandwich out on Sheep or a deviled egg at *The Cobbler's*. More often than not, Rosie would honor a family tradition by lightening the day with an "Elevensie" or a "Nooner". Her nephew, the playwright Richard Dresser, captured this midday ritual in his play, *Wonderful World*:

> LYDIA: Well, as long as you're here would you get me a glass of ice water?
>
> (Max goes to the bar. A second clock chimes. He works through the following, responding to his mother's requests.)
>
> LYDIA (continuing): You can skip the water, dear, just ice in a glass would be enchanting. (Pause.) And you might liven it up with a hint of vermouth, if it's not a bother? Thank you. (Pause.) You know, just a tiny little splash of gin with the vermouth would be delightful. (Pause.) Oh, let's just forget the silly vermouth. And the ice. If it's no trouble.
>
> (Max brings his mother a glass of straight gin.)
>
> MAX: No trouble at all Mother. Here's your ice water.
>
> LYDIA: Thank you, dear. Sure you won't join me, as long as you dropped by at cocktail hour?
>
> MAX: It's two o'clock. I have to get back to school.

Following lunch—with or without an "Elevensie"—there would be a brief nap, followed by a sail, another row, perhaps another mountain climb or some other diversion like tea at Jordan Pond. Cocktails would begin the moment the "sun was over the yard arm", usually accompanied by croquet or Whiffleball. Children drank Shirley Temples from long glasses. Supper was around eight, so the cocktail "hour" was generously measured. It was a cheery, inclusive time of day—an opportunity to tell and retell and tell once again many of the same family stories that had been told to earlier generations. The stories were told with such vitality and color—such immediacy—that it took more than a few of the children years to realize that most of the tales involved long dead eighteenth and early nineteenth century ancestors, not contemporaries.

Much of Rosie's time was also devoted to local organizations. When the Somes House was closed and sold in 1963 to the Haynes family of Millbrook, New York, the future of the town landing was in jeopardy. For decades, the Somes House had operated the private landing as a public service for the local community. Suddenly public access to the harbor was in jeopardy. Rosie teamed up with her close friends Bob Patterson, Reggie Allen and several others to form the Somesville Landing Corporation which acquired the landing, and has operated it ever since for the benefit of Somesville residents. In addition to serving as its sometime president, Rosie for many years was in charge of fund raising. At least one week each summer was dedicated to addressing and stuffing envelopes with the annual appeal for funds.

In the 1970s, Mount Desert, generally, and Somesville, more particularly, began to change. The OPEC oil shock and the stagflation that followed was a catalyst. Attendance at Acadia National Park spiked up when people who several years earlier might happily have driven west to Yosemite or Yellowstone discovered that one of the country's finest national parks was just six hours from Boston. During the 1960s, approximately two million visitors entered Acadia annually. In 1972, that figure jumped twenty-five percent. By the end of the decade, Acadia was attracting four million visitors each year, most of whom came during the two hectic months of July and August. The Park Service effectively handled the growth within Acadia itself, but the access roads were never designed to handle millions of visitors. Major bottlenecks began to develop at the entrance to the island, and Somesville's once quiet main street became either a traffic jam or a speedway depending on the time of day.

But more than the traffic patterns were changing in Somesville. After ninety-three years at their original site, the Fernalds moved their general store from the center of Somesville to an increasingly busy intersection on the outskirts of the village which enabled them to capture traffic on the way to Northeast Harbor as well as Southwest. The Post Office also moved from the center of the village to a spanking new building opposite the busier-than-ever Fernald's store. Rosie could no longer walk across the street to buy a roast or walk two houses over to mail a letter. Although Somesville retained its elegant strip of nineteenth century houses, it no longer felt like a village. There was no commercial pulse, no place to informally gather, no visible sense of community.

The move by Fernald's was more than geographic. It was culinary as well. The quality of the stock was quickly downgraded in order to accommodate campers and other short-term visitors. The butcher was gone, and so were the delicacies. In fact, gasoline rather than food was the prime product. This was commercially shrewd, but it meant that Rosie now had to drive to the Pine Tree Market in Northeast or to Sawyers in Southwest to buy the higher quality foods she had once been able to get across the street. In Somesville, Victor and Ruby Higgins' store just down the street from Rosie had as much charm as the original Fernald's, but not the scope. The market in Somesville had changed, in every sense of the word.

And, of course, the people were changing, too. Bob Fernald, John Fernald, Frances Manning, Margaret Ayer Barnes, indeed, most of the principal characters in these fourteen letters were dead by 1980. So were Rosie's mother and her two uncles, Dan and George Lincoln, each of whom had figured, in one way or another, in Rosie's acquisitions of *The Cobbler's* and, later, Sheep Island. Her brother Waldo had suffered a debilitating stroke landing his sailing dinghy, *Pleione,* at the Somesville town landing, and her sister Louisa developed such severe rheumatoid arthritis that she was confined to a wheelchair and no longer visited Somesville. Friends like Helen Howe and George Mikhalapov had died early, one of cancer, the other in a tragic driving accident. Summer stalwarts of the 1950s and earlier like the Gilpins, the Disstons and the Gilpatrics were largely gone. Old Somesville friends like Bunny and Anne Barnes, Ed and Mary Barnes, Reggie Allen and Danny and Alida Davis came for short visits rather than long, leisurely stays.

The death, on April 6, 1979, of John Fernald, Rosie's guiding spirit in restoring *The Cobbler's*, was especially sad. She would have agreed with columnist Doris Grant who wrote in the *Bar Harbor Times* that, "with the passing of John Fernald there is another break in the family circle, but there is also a break in that friendly circle that encompasses the village and the island community." This lovable, gruff, bear of a man had been Rosie's guide and protector as she embarked on the restoration of *The Cobbler's*. As importantly, he was an early window into the local community she had grown to love.

Several times during the 1970s, Rosie drove further east in search of villages and houses that reminded her of Somesville and *The Cobbler's* as she had found them in 1947. Corea, an austere fishing village on the eastern shore of Schoodic Peninsula, and Cutler, a charming village with a deepwater harbor at the tip of the long peninsula below Machias, were two leading prospects. The tides in each were strong, the air deep with fish and pine. There were a few summer residents, but local rules and character held sway, something that always appealed to Rosie about Somesville. She looked at several houses with the quixotic hope of recreating her magical summer of 1947. But Rosie was no longer a thirty-eight year old just home from the war. She was well into her sixties, and had far too many friends on Mt. Desert, summer and local, to realistically consider starting over.

Part of Rosie's wandering further downeast was frustration with the traffic and development on Mt. Desert. Part of it was pure restlessness. Well into her late seventies, she possessed—or was possessed by—a cyclonic energy that had increasingly few outlets. Her acting and directing career at the Foothills Theater in Worcester and her manic, three state social life were fulfilling but insufficient. In particularly restless moments, Rosie would ruminate on one of the few clear regrets in her life: missing the chance to buy the Somes House when it was going out of business in the early 1960s. Owning and operating a vintage hotel would have combined her interests and talents uncommonly well. The mix of theater, business, architecture, sociability, commitment to a "right way to do things" and, in the case of the Somes House, one of the finest views on the island, were an irresistible draw and Rosie knew it. A distant cousin of hers had very successfully returned the Claremont Hotel in Southwest Harbor to its nineteenth century glory, and Rosie

The Somes House with its graceful porch and nineteenth century ambience (1950s)

would loved taking a crack at doing the same with the Somes House. If her generous uncle, George Lincoln, had died a year earlier, she most likely would have done it.

Much as they loved its setting, most of Rosie's nephews and nieces eventually viewed this barely missed opportunity to buy the Somes House as a golden bullet dodged. Instead of making their respective ways as editors, lawyers, playwrights, teachers, social workers and bankers, their professional careers would have been devoted to making beds, cleaning bathrooms, waiting on table, bookkeeping and spending hour upon hour folding sheets in the hotel laundry. Good jobs as teenagers, they would have pinched the lives of thirty year olds itching to see the world.

Much as Rosie loved the "old Somesville", she did not revel in its past. She had had enough of "the past" growing up. In 1971, she went to a cocktail party in Boston given by a retired Winsor teacher whom she pulled aside and asked, "What's the pension like?" He looked at her with surprise and said, "You just drank it!" Hearing that and feeling more than a little exhausted by the culture wars of the late 1960s, Rosie retired from Winsor in 1973 at the age of sixty-three. Her initial plan was to spend the better part of the year in Somesville, but financial caution, apprehension about lonely winters, and an untamable work ethic soon led her to the newly formed Foothills Theater Company in Worcester where she worked as an actress and director during the next sixteen years.

In a *Worcester Telegram* profile summing up her career at Foothills, Rosie told reporter Frank Magiera, "When I began . . . I played a lot of elderly drunks . . . Then I went through a period when I was playing royalty, queen of all the Russias and all that. Then, for some reason, I was doing lots of mothers. Maybe I'll go out playing a string of ingénues." Although acting—on and off the stage—was certainly in her blood, directing was her real gift. Every year at Winsor, she had directed the eighth grade class in a production of Shakespeare. Virginia Wing, the head of the school and a dear friend to Rosie, wrote in a Winsor tribute that:

> Few teachers have so instinctively understood the creative process. Few have realized so completely how important to young people is the appeal of the imagination, and no one has learned how to elicit so adroitly the best performance from them.

In a 2004 *Winsor Bulletin* dedicated to "Unforgettable Teachers", Constance Brown recalled that Rosie "urged us to look beyond the expected":

> She expected eighth graders to be able to understand Shakespeare and relish performing his work, and under her guidance we did . . . Class VIII put on its own play, which the students chose. Miss Dresser convened a meeting at her home of a group of seniors, and went over suggested plays with us. She wanted us—in 1966, when we were not yet paying attention to the war in Vietnam, but obviously she was—to choose Euripides' *The Trojan Women*. We didn't, but once again she was challenging us.

Although Rosie confessed to the *Telegram* reporter that after twenty-five years she had finally "got to the point that

RLD with Winsor students in the assembly hall later named in her honor (1961)

if I ever saw another child in Shakespearian tights, I think I'd vomit", her years teaching bright women at Winsor were deeply satisfying. Doubtless, she saw much of herself in her young students and held them to the same daunting standards she held for herself. Thankfully, she was much less demanding of her nephews and nieces.

On retiring from Winsor in 1973, Rosie was delighted to return to the professional stage at Foothills where, among other productions, she directed *The Diary of Anne Frank*, *A Moon for the Misbegotten* and *The Taming of the Shrew.* Rosie also made several directorial returns to Winsor where she had been elected a life member of the Corporation in 1977. As an alternative to vomiting at the sight of "another child in Shakespearian tights", she particularly enjoyed directing her fully-grown eighth graders in Winsor's 1988 *Wing Ding*, and in playing Miss Winsor, herself, in

RLD posing as Mary Pickard Winsor at the Winsor Centennial beside the author's mother-in-law and Miss Winsor's great niece, Hope Trumbull Moore (1986)

the 1986 *Centennial Review*. She enjoyed playing roles that celebrated friends and institutions she admired—in 1978 she portrayed her friend Alice Higgins in *The Three Phases of Alice*, a tribute to the latter's long service as chairman of the Clark University Board of Trustees. In summing up Rosie's theatrical career, the *Worcester Telegram* headline got it right: "Rose Dresser Does What She Loves Best."

Rosie's move in the 1970s from Winsor to Foothills gave her far more flexibility in managing her life, and she began staying in Somesville from early May through October. She made new friends like Stanley and Leila Bright on Islesford, Rosilla Breed in Manset, and her new neighbors across the street in Somesville, Don and Beth Straus, whom she was delighted to see take such spirited and enlightened care

Playbills from productions at the Casino Carousel in Bar Harbor, featuring RLD (1950)

of the old Somes House property. Rosie gave up all-day hikes over Sargent and Jordan mountains in favor of more leisurely walks around Jordan Pond and Eagle Lake or along the carriage trails, especially around Parkman Mountain and Hadlock Pond. She was more inclined to take a swim in the bright, Hockney-colored pool at the Harbor Club than in the chilly waters of Somes Harbor. She spent fewer nights alone out on Sheep. She began having Zelig-like encounters with celebrated summer visitors—dinner in Somes Harbor with Malcolm Forbes on his boat the *Highlander*; cocktails with Casper and Jane Weinberger; dinner with Norman Mailer whom she both flustered and charmed by asking, "Mailer, Why do I know that name? What exactly is it that you do?"

Fall became her favorite time of year. The island shifted into much lower gear after Labor Day. Rosie could spend more time with her local friends. Although the "originals"—John Fernald, June Smith, Frances Manning—had died, she loved spending time with people like Steve Hansen, the Somesville harbor master, and Don Smith, who helped her take care of Sheep Island and *The Cobbler's.* Old friends like Ed and Mary Barnes began coming for longer vacations each September, and Rosie had more time to spend hiking with newer friends like Leila Bright and Ruth Fraley.

RLD and Bob Patterson in the distant "wake of the coasters"—Don and Beth Straus (early 1980s)

Well into her seventies, she still loved a sporting challenge. Rosie and her neighbors across the street, Don and Beth Straus, owned identical Jarvis Newman rowboats, and for several years they staged a rowing race from Bar Island at the mouth of Somes Harbor to the Somesville Landing. Rosie's partner was Bob Patterson, then in his eighties, but a former stroke of the Harvard crew. Although the Strauses won every race—gracefully and by wide margins—Rosie and Bob took some solace that they got more exercise by refusing to follow their competitors simple strategy of rowing the straightest course from start to finish. The contestants wore comic hats—Rosie's and Bob's read: "S.S. Repuls've"—that got the attention of cruisers in the harbor who had anchored in Somesville expecting quiet and peace. The still morning air was soon disturbed by shrill, spontaneous blasts of boat horns from spectators who quickly got into the spirit of the race.

As Rosie spent more time in Somesville in the 1970s and 1980s and as the village and island changed, she emerged as something of a *de facto* bridge, a bit of human glue, between some of the complex social groupings on the island. Not unlike micro-climates, groups on Mt. Desert could be moments away physically, but worlds apart otherwise: local and summer people; older money and newer money; money and no money; hikers and sailors; spenders and savers; older summer people and newer ones; social bees and Quietsiders; plutocrats and the occasional democrat. As close friend or recent acquaintance, Rosie found a common ground with an astonishing range of people. She was as engaged talking to Steve Hansen, the harbormaster, or Stan and Binny MacDonald, her civic-minded neighbors, as she was talking to off-islanders such as August Heckscher, the printer and New York City Parks Commissioner or Nathan Pusey, the university president. She had particularly close friends on the Cranberry Islands, Seal Harbor, Hulls Cove and Southwest Harbor as well as in Somesville. She took great pleasure in keeping these groups informally networked together.

In the early 1980s Louisa, suffering from acute rheumatoid arthritis, gave her half interest in *The Cobbler's* and

Sheep Island to her seven nephews and nieces who joined with Rosie in forming the Sheep Island Trust to preserve the two properties. Twenty years later the trust is going strong and the children of Waldo and Frannie, Rosie's nephews and nieces, make full use of *The Cobbler's* and Sheep Island each summer. Their children—for whom this book is largely intended—represent the fifth generation to spend part of their summers on Mt. Desert. But things do change. When John Curtis, a childhood friend of Rosie's, dropped by unannounced one afternoon at *The Cobbler's* he reported, "The house is under very different management!" If cleanliness really is next to godliness, Rosie's nieces and nephews are headed for Dante's *Purgatorio.* Under Rosie, *The Cobbler's* was *Paradiso*.

In her last years, Rosie became uncharacteristically reflective, especially when she was in Somesville and especially about her experiences during the war. One Columbus Day weekend in the early 1980s she was having cocktails with a nephew in the front parlor of *The Cobbler's*. John Fernald's Franklin stove was lit, and the sun was setting on an iron-cold fall day. The tide was slowly filling the cove in front of the house. Scotch in hand, Rosie talked for nearly three hours—a slow soliloquy—about the war.

The performance began modestly with a jovial account of her convincing the Red Cross in Washington to take her on as a volunteer in Europe. She told familiar tales of meeting childhood friends like Paul Morgan, George Bullock and Waite Hurlburt in London for drinks and the theater on their frequent leaves from the military. It sounded like fun.

History of the 12th Evacuation Hospital

D-Day: Planes and gliders flying directly over RLD's hospital in the south of England (June 6, 1944)

But Rosie's tone began to change as she described the troop build-up in the late spring of 1944. Her diction became sharper, her pauses longer, her eyes more distant. It was as if she were describing events that had happened moments ago, not decades. She described a chance encounter with her brother, Waldo, on a Coast Guard cruiser docked in the south of England two days before the Normandy invasion. He could only talk briefly, because he and his shipmates had strict orders to stay aboard ship, preferably below deck. Rosie mimicked her fleeting encounter with Waldo, acting as if he were just across the room. In fact, it was their hurried conversation that tipped Rosie that the long rumored Allied invasion of Europe was about to begin. She knew instinctively that the months of waiting were over. Security was tighter, tempers were shorter. Something was up.

And she was right. Two days after seeing Waldo, Rosie was one of the few people awake in a field hospital outside of

Weymouth as the first waves of American warplanes began thundering directly overhead. D-Day had arrived. As Rosie talked, there was relief in her voice, even exhilaration, as she sat in her wing chair remembering one of the most dramatic moments in her life.

Rosie's description of following Patton's Third Army across France and Belgium towards Germany was more rambling and disjoint. That was probably just as Rosie experienced it —anecdotes without context, motion without a real sense of direction or progress. She told a story about an accordionist playing one evening for the wounded Allied soldiers in a hospital near the fast moving front. One ward of badly injured and emotionally dispirited soldiers listened with sullen indifference as the musician tried to cheer them up. Not succeeding, he finished his last tune, and began packing up his instrument to move on to another floor. Just as he was leaving the darkened ward, an injured soldier asked him to play "God Bless America". The accordionist quickly unpacked his instrument and started to play. As he did, the entire floor of seemingly broken men began singing. Rosie said it was the first time she had really understood the power of a song. As she finished the story, her eyes glistened uncharacteristically with tears. Even her nephew, brought up as he was in the anti-heroic Vietnam era, was startled by the emotional resonance.

Night had long fallen and, at some point during the evening, Rosie must have gotten up to pour herself another Scotch—or, more likely, asked her nephew to do so. In any event, she continued her soliloquy. After talking reverentially about Patton—with a tone and categorical respect that did not come naturally to her—she switched gears. Her voice softened, but her body seemed to tighten. She began talking about her experience dealing with emaciated survivors in one of the Austrian death camps towards the end of the war. She did not name the camp, but it must have been in the Mauthausen complex near Linz.

Despite seeing some of the worst combat cases in the 12th Evacuation Hospital earlier in the war, Rosie said she was completely unprepared for what she saw in Linz. The survivors were barely more than living dead—starved, desiccated bodies staring wide-eyed at nothing. A number died after the camp was liberated, but others were saved by patiently getting liquids into their dehydrated bodies. Many could not swallow water directly, and were placed in baths to absorb whatever liquids they could. Rosie's description was visceral, precise, quiet and brief. Other than saying it was the saddest and worst thing she had seen in her life, Rosie did not linger. She moved on with her story for another half hour or so—volunteering for the Pacific, wasting time in the Philippines, deciding to return to the United States rather than visit occupied Japan. It was a thin dénouement to the story of Linz, a recovered memory that had drained her. The evening ended. Tired, she slipped off to bed. Hungry and a bit overwhelmed, the nephew headed off to the icebox.

It was the first time he had heard Rosie talk about the death camps. As far as he knew, she had not spoken about them to anyone else, although she soon did so with several others including a nurse. In a newspaper interview with the

Worcester Telegram in the summer of 1945, Rosie had said that a number of camp survivors had "passed through the 121st Evacuation Hospital" but the reporter noted that, "Miss Dresser did not come in contact with them." Although the interview has some lighthearted touches, the dark gravity of war permeates. The reporter observed that Rosie, "Is reluctant to speak of her experiences. Obviously, she has seen much of the war at an evacuation hospital which handled operative cases." None of her war letters home mentions the camps, even in the most oblique way. Of course, her letters were censored, but it remains intriguing—though not surprising—that such deep and emotionally disturbing experiences could be so fully suppressed for so long.

Rosie's final years were medically and psychologically difficult. She was a purebred who loved to run at her own fast pace without some thinly framed jockey telling her where to go, when, or how fast. She hated being dependent on others, but as she deteriorated physically she had no choice. Even though she had given up smoking over thirty years earlier, she developed progressively acute emphysema. Her Pall Malls had left a fatal legacy.

In the late fall of 1989, and somewhat incredibly given her difficulty breathing, Rosie began directing *The Diary of Anne Frank* at the Worcester Foothills Theater. It was likely to be her last play, something even she seemed to acknowledge. Early into the casting and first readings of the play, it became clear that she was too weak to continue. Rosie knew the play itself must go on, but that she—at eighty and chronically short of breath—could not. The producers, Marc and Susie Smith, handled an awkward situation gracefully. Rosie would take a break, a replacement would be hired and she would do another show later in the year. But her family —and, perhaps, even Rosie herself—knew that her theatrical career had come to an end.

The spring of 1990 was especially tough. She had sold her house in Woodstock to a nephew several years earlier, and had moved into an apartment in the back of John and Frannie Herron's house in downtown Worcester. The apartment had been decorated with many of her prizes—a lush Frank Benson portrait of Aunt Dorothy Lincoln; two mid-eighteenth century embroideries, one of a family house, Chandler Farms, in Pomfret, Connecticut; a walnut rocker, upholstered in blood-red velvet that had belonged to Levi Lincoln II, governor of Massachusetts; elegantly bound and mostly unread books belonging to Arthur Sherburne Hardy, minister to Spain; an overhead photograph of Sheep Island taken from a plane; pictures of her great nieces and nephews hamming it up. Putting her best spin on it, she told a friend, "Life is great. I have a new oxygen tank, a new VCR and a new bottle of Scotch." As ever, she tried to put the brightest face on things.

But the move was not a success. However elegant the apartment might appear to visitors, it was a dungeon to Rosie. As the Mt. Desert author, Marguerite Yourcenar, had Hadrian recall, "That palace of Antioch where I was to live some years later in a virtual frenzy of delight, was for me, but a prison, and perhaps a death cell." Rosie felt trapped in a gilded cage. She ached to get to Maine, flush as it was with raw, clean air for her emphysema and for the final vestige of independence it offered her flagging spirits.

The summer of 1991, seventy-nine years after her first summer in Seal Harbor, would be her last on Mt. Desert. She traveled downeast by ambulance as her mother had a quarter century earlier. Two attendants were with her full-time. Her nephews, nieces and sole surviving sibling, Frannie, and her husband, John, visited her during the summer. Rosie's bristling energy was gone, but she made a gallant effort to keep the social ball spinning. At cocktail hour, whenever the weather was clear, Rosie was driven by one of her nurses to Seawall, a stone beach beyond Manset that looked out on a stark ocean that stretched, as she liked to say, all the way to Brazil. She would sit in a plastic lawn chair and slowly sip a glass of Scotch as she stared in silent reverie at the waves crashing in front of her.

If a nephew or niece or old friend were with her at Seawall, Rosie would make eye contact and struggle to be the host that she had spent the better part of her life being. But the hollowness in her eyes, her tiny gulps of air, her shrinking physique betrayed her. She was mortally sick. No quick smile, no elegant tweed jacket, no entourage could hide that. It was her last summer in Maine.

On returning to Worcester, she moved into a nursing home. Her sister and brother-in-law's apartment was too much for her, even with nurses and companions. Rosie deteriorated quickly, and by Christmas she was transferred to the Memorial Hospital. On December 25, her sister, Frannie, and a nephew visited her after a long Christmas dinner

Cocktail hour at Seawall: RLD and her nephews, Richard Dresser and the author during RLD's final summer on Mt. Desert (1991)

with the Dresser and Herron families at *Buttercupthorpe*, the Waldo Dresser house in nearby Jefferson. Rosie had a mad, Shakespearean look—crazed, anxious, possessed. She was haunted, and she was haunting. Her powerful, imperious bearing had vaporized. Once nearly six feet, she was shriveled, frail and tiny as a vulnerable hatchling.

But Rosie was not about to die easily. She battled the inevitable for another week until her life-saving oxygen tanks were rendered useless by the fluids intractably filling her lungs. She finally drowned in her hospital bed on New Year's Eve, a miserable death for a proud woman.

Her funeral was held in Worcester on January 10, 1992 at the First Unitarian Church, a church founded by her ancestors nearly two hundred years earlier. The austere building with its stately columns and Wren-like steeple is perched on Court Hill, a bluff adjacent to the County Courthouse overlooking Lincoln Square, the epicenter of a long forgotten "Old Worcester". Several hundred mourners celebrated the many phases of a life that began in the distant afterglow of what Van Wyck Brooks called New England's "Indian Summer" and traversed the better part of a violent century.

Her life had begun in unearned privilege—governesses, a mansion house, travel abroad, ancestral reveries, summers in Maine—and evolved into one of well-earned accomplishment. As an actress and teacher she made her way in the Depression. As a Red Cross volunteer, she witnessed first-hand the coarse savagery of World War II. Despite dropping out of Vassar and never earning a college degree, she became the assistant head of a distinguished secondary school in Boston. She acted and directed into her eighties. She presided over organizations—the Players Club, the Shakespeare Club, the Somesville Landing Corporation, the Somesville Village Improvement Society, to name a few—in different cities, at different times. She traveled frequently abroad and was always enamored with islands, especially Sicily and the Orkneys. She had friends—from childhood, from Vassar, from the war, from the theater, from Winsor—whom she kept up with all her life. She ran into them all the time—on trains bound for Florence, on the hiking trails of Mt. Desert, in ice cream shops along the Maine Turnpike, on the streets of New York—in a way that seemed statistically improbable until one remembered how many people she knew and how memorable she was. She hated being alone, and seldom was.

A unifying theme of the funeral and the reception

Rose Lincoln Dresser (1986)

afterwards was Rosie's love of Maine. Captivated as she was by an abiding sense of place, Rosie was never more at home than when she was in residence at *The Cobbler's* or out on Sheep Island. Mt. Desert managed to capture the diverse and colorful threads of her life and cobble them into a meaningful whole. Her childhood was omnipresent, especially in the fields across the street from *The Cobbler's* and in the presence of old friends from distant summers. Vassar roommates and friends summered nearby, as did her close friend from the war, Lettie Jones Crosby. Former Winsor students and their parents were similarly close at hand, although this became a mixed blessing when the stresses of the late 1960s wore Rosie's patience thin. Friends from Worcester, Cambridge, Woodstock and most all compass points arrived in Somesville throughout the summer for weekends that shook the ancient foundations of her small house. Local friends—the postmaster, the grocer, the caretaker, the harbormaster—kept her grounded in an otherwise precious world. Physically, the island triggered memories of favorite places like the Orkneys, Crete, the Lake District, even Venice where Rosie thought a *vaporetto* ride to the Lido on a brilliant day was like taking the ferry from Northeast Harbor to Little Cranberry as boats sped madly between glistening islands.

In her eulogy, The Reverend Barbara Merritt closed by quoting from a tape recording of Barbara Cooney's *Miss Rumphius* made by Rosie for her great-nephew, Sam Truesdell. Imagining, Rosie's precise and resonant voice:

> My great-aunt Alice, Miss Rumphius, is very old now. Her hair is very white . . . they call her the Lupine Lady. Sometimes my friends stand with me outside her gate, curious to see the old, old lady who planted the fields of lupines . . . They think she is the oldest woman in the world. Often she tells us stories of faraway places. "When I grow up," I tell her, "I, too, will go to far away places and come home to live by the sea."

This is a conversation that Rosie, a world traveler and lover of lupines, might well have had with her own aunts, great and otherwise. She actively instilled those sentiments in her nieces and nephews, great-nephews and great-nieces. And, indeed, many of them have traveled to "far away places" and most find time each summer to "come home to live by the sea."

RLD *and her nephew* Richard Dresser *contemplating "far away places" at Seawall (1954)*

"On the 26th of December, 1950, on an evening of freezing cold and in the almost polar silence of Mount Desert Island, off the Atlantic shore, I was striving to live again through the smothering heat of a day in July, in the year 138 in Baiae, to feel the weight of a sheet on weary, heavy limbs, and to catch the barely perceptible sound of that tideless sea as from time to time it reached a man whose whole attention was concentrated upon other murmurs, those of his approaching death. I tried to go as far as the last sip of water, the last spasm of pain, the last image in his mind. Now the emperor had but to die."

Marguerite Yourcenar, "Reflections on the Composition", *Memoirs of Hadrian*

AFTERWORD & ACKNOWLEDGEMENTS

The opportunity to take fourteen letters written by Rosie Dresser during the summer of 1947 and build a story around them hardly compares to the majestic and brilliantly realized leap taken by Margeuerite Yourcenar, the Somesville author, who wrote her masterpiece, *Memoirs of Hadrian* on Mt. Desert. But the forensic standard Yourcenar set—going "as far as the last sip of water, the last spasm of pain"—was liberating. As I gazed out from my office looking over Seal Harbor and absorbed her challenge, I knew I was not up to it. Not even close. Getting *inside* Rosie's head was far beyond my talent. When a Winsor graduate asked me years ago whether Rosie had ever had a lover, I was stumped. Dumbfounded. Clueless. I had no idea. Did she ever have sex? No idea. Why didn't she marry? It wasn't, as she jokingly claimed, because, Lincolns always marry above themselves and she never met anyone better. I simply do not know. In writing this short account, all I have tried to do—at best, all I have done—is to tell the outline of her story based on external evidence rather than internal speculation. As the science scholar Leslie Paul deftly put it, I have simply been "rummaging around in the rag bag of observed facts." But it's been fun.

Along the way, numerous good friends and generous acquaintances have given advice, offered warnings, made introductions, improved my grammar, and most importantly been enthusiastic supporters of a quixotic undertaking. Among others, they include: David Korzenik, Eric Rayman, Alex Gibney, Betsy West, Tony King, Susie Reed, John Jeppson, Susie Marsh and Don and Beth Straus. Jane Hoeffel Otte, the archivist of the Winsor School, Wayne Kempton, the archivist of the Epicopal Diocese of New York and the librarians at the Jesup Library in Bar Harbor, Maine were helpful in providing, respectively, photographs of Rosie, Bishop Manning and micro-film of *The Bar Harbor Times*. George Dresser, my co-trustee of the family archives, has shown remarkable patience and flexibility in "keeping everything together". I owe the greatest practical thanks to Ingrid Mach, the talented and hardworking book designer who transformed my overly formatted Word files into a highly professional looking book. Nothing starts so literally with a blank piece of paper—or, nowadays, a blank Word file—as a book. Ingrid's gift for using abstract "bits and bytes" to realize the tactile possibilities of paper, ink and cardboard have made this a far better looking book than it deserves to be. My brother Frank did a wonderful job as a last minute editor. His sharp eye and thorough reading made this a much better book. The reporters at the *Post Herald* in Syracuse are in good hands but I would not want to be one of his Newhouse students. Thanks also to Kathy Michie at Mercantile-Image Press for her cheerful advice and the professionalism of her entire team.

Finally, and most importantly, I want to thank Julia Moore and our son Levi—the former for her good natured forbearance and consistent encouragement, the latter for his benevolent indifference—in letting me steal away so much family time to complete this book. I had no idea that an accidental discovery on a rainy spring morning of a misplaced file in a large archive could lead me down such an all-consuming path. Three years later, I now know.

Bibliography and Sources

LINCOLN-DRESSER FAMILY ARCHIVES: The fourteen letters written by Rosie to her family during the summer of 1947 are drawn from the Lincoln-Dresser Family Archives, a seventy-thousand piece collection in Worcester, MA. So are a number of other letters cited including several written by Rosie during the war and two her sister Louisa wrote during a curatorial trip through the Middle East in 1938. The archives were the source of articles quoted from the *Worcester Telegram*, the *Worcester Evening Gazette*, the *Bar Harbor Times* and the *Winsor School Newsletter* (Spring 1992 and the *Winsor Bulletin* (Winter-Spring 2004).

MAINE: Allen, Richard and Mazlish, Ann; *Somesville: Self-Guided Tour*; Mt. Desert Historical Society, 1995. Caldwell, Bill; *Islands of Maine: Where America Really Began*; Downeast Books, Camden, ME; 1981. Hansen, Gunnar (editor); *Mount Desert, An Informal History*; Town of Mount Desert, ME; 1989. Martin, Clara Barnes; *Guide Book for Mount Desert*; Loring Short & Harmon, Portland, ME; sixth edition; 1885. Sanderson, Virginia Somes; *The Living Past*; Beech Hill Publishing Company, Mt. Desert, ME; 1982. Thornton,

Mrs. Seth; *Tradition and Records: Southwest Harbor and Somesville*; 50th Anniversary Edition, Acadia Publishing, Bar Harbor, ME; 1988. Tracy, Charles; *The Tracy Log Book* (edited by Ann Mazlish); Acadia Publishing Company, Bar Harbor, ME; 1997. Wilmerding, John; *The Artist's Mount Desert*; Princeton University Press, Princeton, NJ; 1994.

World War II: Brackman, Arnold C.; *The Other Nuremberg: The Untold Story of the Tokyo War Crimes Trials*; Quill/William Morrow, New York, NY; 1987. Fussell, Paul; *The Boys Crusade: The American Infantry in Northwestern Europe, 1944-1945;* The Modern Library, New York; 2003. Morse, Ralph; "George Lott, Casualty", *Life Magazine* January 29, 1945. Origo, Iris; *War in Val D'Orcia: An Italian War Diary ~ 1943-44*; David Godine, Boston; 2000. Shacklette, Hansford T.; *History of the 12th Evacuation Hospital: 25 August, 1942 – 25 August 1945*; Sebaldus-Verlag, Nurnberg, 1945.

Lincoln-Dresser Family: Brooke, John L.; *The Heart of the Commonwealth; Society and Political Culture in Worcester County* 1713-1861, Cambridge University, Cambridge, UK; 1989. Dresser, Richard W.; *Wonderful World*; Dramatic Publishing, Woodstock, IL; 2002; World premiere production at the Actor's Theater of Louisville's 25 Annual Humana Festival of New American Plays on March 16, 2001. Flexner, James Thomas; *Maverick's Progress: An Autobiography*; Fordham University Press, New York, NY; 1996. Herron, Frances M.; "The Lincoln House", *Marvelous Messages*; Privately printed, Worcester, MA; 1975. Southwick, Albert; "Flowers of Old Worcester: The Dresser Sisters –Frances, Louisa and Rose",

Worcester Magazine; February 1995. Lincoln, Waldo; *The History of the Lincoln Family*; Commonwealth Press, Worcester, MA 1923. Woodstock Hill Study Group; *Woodstock Hill: Historic District Study*; Woodstock, CT; 1995.

OTHER: Jewett, Sarah Orne; "A White Heron", *Novels and Stories;* Library of America. Lively, Penelope; *A House Unlocked*; Grove Press, 2001. Lowell, Robert, "Fourth of July", *Near the Ocean*; Farrar, Straus & Giroux. Wilde, Oscar; *The Importance of Being Earnest and Other Plays*; Signet Classic, 1985. Yourcenar, Marguerite; *Memoirs of Hadrian*, "Reflections on the Composition"; Farrar, Straus, Giroux, 1963.

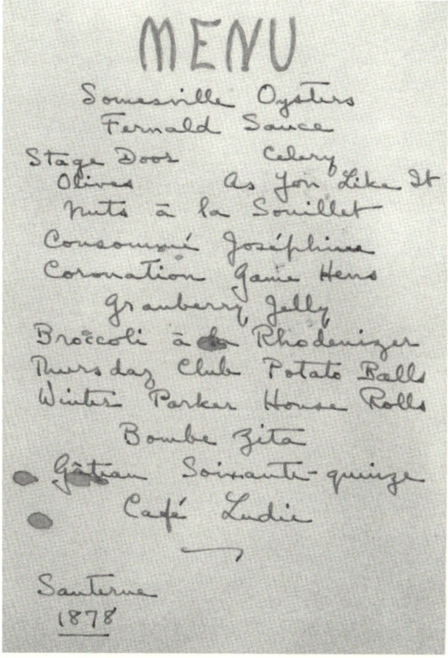

Celebrating Ga's 75th birthday at The Cobbler's *(late 1950s)*

The dock at Sheep Island: high tide, flag hoisted, southwesterly blowing, the Lincoln D *and* Pleione *secure, RLD's brother-in-law John Herron walking up the gangway—life goes on (early 1990s)*